Making Lemonade

Making Lemonade

A Bright View on Investing, on Financial Markets, and on the Economy

Martin L. Mazorra, CFP, CHFC

iUniverse, Inc.
Bloomington

Making Lemonade
A Bright View on Investing, on Financial Markets, and on the Economy

iUniverse books may be ordered through booksellers or by contacting:

iUniverse
1663 Liberty Drive
Bloomington, IN 47403
www.iuniverse.com
1-800-Authors (1-800-288-4677)

Because of the dynamic nature of the Internet, any web addresses or links contained in this book may have changed since publication and may no longer be valid. The views expressed in this work are solely those of the author and do not necessarily reflect the views of the publisher, and the publisher hereby disclaims any responsibility for them.

Any people depicted in stock imagery provided by Thinkstock are models, and such images are being used for illustrative purposes only.

Certain stock imagery © Thinkstock.

ISBN: 978-0-5954-2083-4 (sc)
ISBN: 978-0-5958-6430-0 (e)

Printed in the United States of America

iUniverse rev. date: 8/17/2012

Acknowledgments

I'd like to give special thanks to the clients I've had the pleasure of working with over the past twenty-two years. Their personal experiences, dreams, aspirations, hopes, and fears inspired what you are about to read. Thanks to my staff and associates, whose support and sincere devotion to our clients' lives has made my experience in the financial services industry truly extraordinary. Thanks also to my parents, Len and Pauline Mazorra, for instilling in me the principle that success in life is measured by what a person gives, not what he receives. And to my boys, Nick and Ryan. I have been blessed with a truly remarkable family—words cannot describe how much they mean to me.

Foreword

Over the past two decades, I have had the pleasure of helping literally hundreds of investors design and maintain their investment portfolios. In the process, I have discovered what I truly believe to be the secret to long-term investment success. Unfortunately, my discovery won't win me the next Nobel Prize in economics, a column in the *Wall Street Journal*, or even a guest spot on one of the financial news networks. It's not some groundbreaking concept or strategy. Quite simply, my theory is that it's not the things successful investors do that make them successful, it's the things they *don't* do that make them successful. By and large, successful long-term investors don't read the *Wall Street Journal* or watch CNBC. They don't panic when the stock market dips. They don't put all their eggs in one basket. They don't chase last year's hottest commodity. And, perhaps most importantly, they don't stray from their long-term investment strategy, even when the going gets tough.

Successful investors are generally humble when it comes to their portfolios. They know what they know, and they know what they don't know. They typically leave the day-to-day management to professionals. In their minds, they are successful when they achieve a long-term financial goal. Perhaps funding their children's or grandchildren's college educations, buying their dream vacation home, or retiring with a comfortable income at precisely the age they had planned. In essence, they measure their success by the extent to which they attain financial freedom, not by the rate of return they've earned over the years.

Sounds easy, doesn't it? The fact is, attaining financial freedom has been very easy for the patient investor described above. But apparently, according to a study performed by research firm Dalbar, Inc.[1], the average investor over the past twenty years has not been as patient as the investors described above. It seems the greatest challenge the average investor faces has always been dealing with his own emotions. He tends to do the things the successful investor doesn't. The Dalbar study suggests that the average investor tends to buy and sell securities at precisely the wrong time, ultimately earning considerably less than the major market averages. According to the study, the average investor's average annual return from 1985 to 2004 was 3.90%, while the Standard and Poor's 500 Stock Index (a market value–weighted index of 500 of the most commonly held blue-chip stocks, considered to be a benchmark for the overall stock market) produced an 11.90% yearly gain for the same time period. How could the average investor have done so poorly compared to the overall market? It's simply because the average investor tends to act on emotion, buying stocks or stock funds only when he perceives that everyone's making money, typically after the market has risen for an extended period, only to sell in a blind panic after stocks suffer the inevitable pullback. And, by the way, the difference between 11.90% and 3.90% compounded annually for a dozen and a half years is a fortune.

This book is a compilation of several years worth of client newsletters on the subjects of investing and the economy. I wrote these brief essays during times of market euphoria and times of despair. My wish for you is that this little book helps you gain what I believe is the proper perspective when it comes to your money—that the glass is always half full, and almost without exception there is a financial bright side to the events and circumstances that shape the financial universe. You'll notice an underlying theme, particularly in the articles on investing, that long-term thinking, patience, and at

---

1 Source: Dalbar Inc., Quantitative Analysis of Investor Behavior, 2005. Represents average annually compounded returns of equity indices vs. equity mutual fund investors; based on the length of time shareholders actually remain invested in a fund and the historical performance of the fund's appropriate index.

times a strong stomach are the key ingredients to investment success. The newsletters are separated into three sections. Sections 1 (Bull Markets) and 2 (Bear Markets) consist of investment topics, separated by the predominant mood of the stock market at that time. Section 3 is devoted to topics related to the economy. Ahead of each essay I offer present-day commentary that often ties a past event illustrated in the newsletter to what's occurring in today's investment world.

CONTENTS

SECTION ONE

Bull Markets

"Time and Diversification," written just after the first quarter of 1996, touches on the advantages of dividing a long-term investment portfolio among various asset classes. The chart comparing a very safe fixed-rate investment to a very volatile but well-diversified portfolio vividly illustrates why patience and diversification are key ingredients to long-term investment success.

Time and Diversification
April 1996

The first three months of 1996 have come and gone, and if you had your money in a stock mutual fund, you likely enjoyed another positive quarter. According to Morningstar Mutual Funds (www. morningstar.com), the total return for the average large cap growth fund was 5.88%, while funds that invest in non-U.S. stocks averaged 5.01%, and small company stock funds returned 5.58%.

Corporate Bond Funds, however, posted a Q1, 1996 decline of 1.51%, according to Morningstar. The bond market began to shake on March 8, when the February non-farm jobs report showed a mammoth increase of over 700,000 new jobs, double what most economists expected. A faster-moving economy evokes fears of inflation, putting upward pressure on interest rates, which in turn causes bond prices to fall.

Stock prices also declined on the job news (higher interest rates mean higher individual and corporate borrowing costs, creating headwinds for the economy) but quickly rebounded based on the assumption that a healthy economy (as long as it's not too healthy) is good for corporate profits and thus good for stock prices.

While I'm no advocate of attempting to time the ups and downs of the stock market, you can make a case for 1996 being another good year due to the upcoming election, steady economic growth, and low interest rates. Or you may argue that stock prices are too high after last year's run-up, and, if you're a timer, its time to sell. In fact, this year looks quite different than 1995 in several ways. Last year the Fed was moving toward lower interest rates but appears to have recently shifted to neutral. Bond yields moved lower in 1995, but lately they've been inching their way back up. And, at the beginning of this year, the stock market was considerably higher than it was a year ago.

So where do we go from here? While we can't know where the market is headed in the short run, we do know that long-term investment success depends on two basic concepts: diversification and a long-term attitude. Diversification means spreading your assets among investments with high risk/high return, moderate risk/moderate return, and low risk/low return characteristics. A long-term attitude simply means not panicking in a down market and understanding that even while pursuing higher-than-inflation returns, downward fluctuation is inevitable.

To make the case for diversification, consider the following question and illustration. How much money would you have 25 years from now if you invest $25,000 in an investment that earns 7% per year, versus spreading the $25,000 among five different investments, one resulting in an entire loss, with the other four ranging from 6% to 12% annually?

Value in 25 years		Value in 25 years	
One Investment:		Five Investments:	
$25,000 @ 7%	$135,686	$5,000 @ total loss	$ 0
		$5,000 @ 6%	$ 21,459
		$5,000 @ 8%	$ 34,242
		$5,000 @ 10%	$ 54,174
		$5,000 @ 12%	$ 85,000
Total	**$135,686**	**Total**	**$194,875**

As you can see, the combination of diversification and long-term thinking (patience) can make a big difference.

"Back to Basics" was intended to provide a brief checklist for the new investor desiring to do things in a fundamentally sound and systematic manner, as well as a reminder to the experienced investor to never ignore the basic building blocks that provide the foundation for a sound long-term investment program. These basic principals are every bit as relevant today as they were back in 1997.

Back to Basics
(Investing Rules of Thumb)
January 1997

Investing for the future can be very intimidating when you consider all there is to consider. For starters, there's a myriad of investment vehicles to choose from: stocks, bonds, real estate, gold, silver, mutual funds, limited partnerships, etc. Then once you decide which types of investments best fit your personality, you have to figure out how much of each to own, when to buy, when to sell, whether to hire help. And what about taxes? I believe virtually anyone can learn enough about the various options to determine the right mix, but I'm afraid there's no legitimate answer to the question of when to buy and when to sell. Even the most famous "experts" have been unable to time the "buys and sells" well enough to consistently earn the best possible returns. Things just change too quickly, and markets don't always react the way you might expect, given a certain set of parameters.

With this in mind, think of the following "Investing Rules of Thumb" as a practical guide to building the proper financial foundation and establishing a long-term investment program.

1. Don't begin your long-term portfolio until your short-term portfolio is in place. In essence, you should keep savings in the bank or a money market fund equal to three to six months of living expenses. Also, be sure to maintain the proper amounts of life, health, casualty, and disability insurance.
2. Don't keep more than you need in short-term savings. You'll pay what we call opportunity cost, which means any

amount you maintain above what's needed for emergencies and upcoming purchases has the opportunity to earn a greater rate of return in your long-term portfolio.

3. Pay off all installment debt (for example, high-interest credit cards, personal loans, high-interest auto loans) with the exception of your mortgage and perhaps very low-interest auto loans before beginning to invest long term. The interest you're paying could very well be more than you you'll earn in your portfolio.

4. If you're young, buy stocks—or, as I prefer, mutual funds that invest in stocks. Although there's no guarantee, history suggests that for patient, long-term investors, the stock market offers excellent growth potential.

    - If you're between the ages of 25 and 35 consider investing 65% to 75% of your long-term portfolio in mutual funds that invest in stocks. You'd buy bonds, government securities and /or CDs with the remaining 25% to 35% .
    - If you're 35 to 45, consider investing 55% to 65% in stock funds and the remainder in bonds, government securities, etc.
    - If you're 45 to 60, consider investing 40% to 50% in stock funds and the remainder in bonds, government securities, etc.
    - If you're 60 or above, consider investing 30% in stocks and 70% in bonds, government securities, etc.

5. Never try to time the stock market. Regardless of what anyone may claim, to date no published study exists that suggests market timers can beat the market consistently over the long term. Stay true to your long term strategy.

6. Accept the inevitable fluctuations of the market and understand that you will experience down years. No one can predict the future. However, studies show that most major market declines in the past were closely followed by new market highs. *Never* bail out of the stock market simply because it's down.

7. Pay yourself first. Estimate how much you'll need to save to reach your goals, and make that your number one monthly expense.

8. Get professional advice. Find a financial professional with a reputation for honesty and integrity. The right professional will be a tremendous asset while you strive to reach your financial objectives.

There may be more to consider, given your personal set of circumstances. But if you start with these simple rules of thumb, you'll be well on your way to reaching your financial goals.

In "Why Buy Bonds," written in the summer of 1997, I reminded my readers that balance is an important component of a properly managed portfolio. As you might imagine, bonds were not at all in vogue in 1997—not while stocks were experiencing an amazing run with seemingly no end in sight. Little did I know that, at that moment, we were just thirty-three months away from the beginning of what turned out to be the worst bear market for stocks in modern history. As stocks retreated, bonds rose, providing a cushion for the well-balanced portfolio.

Why Buy Bonds?
June 1997

Why should investors hold a position in bonds as part of their long-term asset allocation program? Now that's a great question, especially when we consider the past. History strongly suggests that over most extended time periods, stocks handily outperform bonds. According to Ibbotson Associates of Chicago's 1997 publication titled "Stocks, Bonds, Bills and Inflation," the Standard & Poor's 500 Stock Index has produced an average annual return of 10.7% since 1926. The Lehman Brothers Long-Term Corp Bond Index (an unmanaged index of long-term U.S. Treasury bonds) has returned just 6.0 % over that same time period. Those of you who've been "in the market" for the past few years would testify that stocks perform better than bonds over the long term, and if you're "in the market," you're most likely a long-term investor. So the question remains, why buy bonds?

In a word: *stability*. While I'll never dispute the fact that stocks over the long term have out-produced bonds, they've done so with greater risk. Risk (or volatility) as measured by standard deviation (the statistical measurement of dispersion around an average, which depicts how widely a stock or portfolio's returns varied over a certain period of time) has been significantly higher for the S&P 500 (20.3% since 1926) than for the LB Corp Bond Index (8.7 % since 1926). This simply means that, historically, stocks have experienced, on average, significantly higher highs and lower lows than bonds.

Let's take a look at a time when holding bonds in a portfolio made great sense: the bear market of 1973 and 1974. This period was characterized by the oil embargo of '73 and the resignation of President Nixon in '74. The chart below illustrates the performance of a $50,000 investment in the S&P 500 Index, the NASDAQ Composite Index (an unmanaged index of U.S. stocks traded on the NASDAQ Over the Counter Exchange), and the LB Corp/Gov't Bond Index for the period beginning 12/31/72 and ending 12/31/75, using CDA Wiesenberger's "wrapper" mutual fund hypothetical software.

End of year	S&P 500	% change	NASDQ	% change	LB Corp/ Gov't bond	% change
12/29/72	$50,000		$50,000		$50,000	
12/31/73	$42,601	-14.8%	$34,934	-30.1%	$51,139	+2.3%
12/31/74	$31,318	-26.5%	$23,100	-33.9%	$51,224	+0.2%
12/31/75	$42,991	+37.3%	$30,466	+31.9%	$57,525	+12.3%
Cumulative return		**-14.02%**		**-39.07%**		**+15.05%**

As you can see, the bond market held up quite well during the early '70s while stocks were getting pummeled across the board.

Now, I'm not predicting a bear market of this magnitude; in fact, I'm not making any prediction whatsoever (we'll leave that to the market "gurus" who usually guess wrong as often as everybody else). I'm simply saying that nothing's for sure in the stock and bond markets, nothing, that is, except volatility. Volatility is a given. The challenge for the investor is to determine his or her comfort level.

Thus, my greatest concern is for the investor who panics and sells his or her holdings when (not if) the market experiences a significant downturn, in essence selling low. Recently I had a conversation with a client who shared with me his mother's unfortunate experience in stocks during the '73–'74 bear market. After losing a large portion of her investment, she got out, vowing never to return. To this day she won't think of devoting even the smallest portion of her portfolio to the stock market. I can't say that if she had the appropriate position in bonds, while stocks were falling, she would feel any differently, but at the very least she would have made some money on a portion of her portfolio during one of the worst periods in stock market history. Of course, if she had hung in there as opposed to selling in a panic, today her stock holdings would have grown to a much larger amount than her bond holdings. Her original investment (as estimated by her son) back in 1973, were it allocated in the same manner as the S&P 500 Index, would have been worth $796,829 by 12/31/96, or $684,692 if it were allocated to a portfolio tracking the NASDAQ Composite Index. While the same investment, allocated to track the Lehman Brothers Corp/Government Bond Index would have grown to $400,043 over the same time period. Obviously it's *time*, not timing, that makes all the difference for the long-term investor.

I wrote "A Dose of Reality" roughly two-thirds into the greatest bull market run of the twentieth century. Optimism was rampant; however, volatility increased as the bull grew older. In late October 1997, the market experienced a severe pullback that caught most investors off guard. I took this opportunity to remind my readers that downward fluctuations are inevitable and that bear markets of more than just a few months are always somewhere in the offing— again, not knowing that the biggest bear market since the Great Depression was just around the corner. Note however that the Dow Jones Industrial Average on October 27, 1997 ended the day at 7,161. Since then, we've experienced a huge three-year sell-off (2000–2002), and lo and behold, the Dow stands today (April 27, 2006) at 11,382—more than 4,000 points higher. Fascinating, isn't it?

The Q and A section of the article offered some insight into the hot topic of that period, the widespread collapse of Asian currencies, along with my perspective on Asia's longer-term outlook.

A Dose of Reality
November 1997

It's the end of the day, October 27, 1997, and the Dow Jones Industrial Average just plunged 554 points, the second biggest one-day point drop and the twelfth biggest percentage drop in the history of the stock market. How did this happen? The market was moving along just fine. We had low interest rates, low inflation, good corporate earnings, lots of cash going to stock funds every month—all the makings of a great outlook for the U.S. stock market. Then "Bloody Monday"! We all thought that, with such a favorable economic backdrop, stocks would just keep moving up indefinitely; after all, it's different this time, right? Well, those who really believed that have just received a dose of some much-needed reality.

You've read here before that I subscribe to the notion that it's next to impossible for anyone to successfully time the market on a consistent basis. Therefore, I expose my own portfolio, and suggest my clients do the same, to the stock markets of the world when a long-term position in equities fits our overall objectives and tolerance for risk, rather than when the "timing" seems right. As a result, at times we feel like geniuses and at other times like nincompoops.

I'm tempted to provide a chart illustrating past down years in the market and the subsequent up years, but you've seen those before. Besides, at this time the Dow is already above where it was before the big sell-off. So can we call this a non-event? Certainly not for that portion of a diversified portfolio allocated to non-U.S. stocks, which are still well below the values seen just a couple of months ago (see Q and A for info on Asian markets). As for our U.S. market, it's easy to blame the October 27 drop on events in Asia (it's widely believed that the massive Asian market sell-off is the primary cause for the recent turmoil in our market). Regardless of where the blame resides, you might say that a Wall Street correction was overdue. Valuations were high relative to historic norms, and next year's corporate earnings outlook isn't as rosy as the past couple of years, particularly if Asia's woes play havoc with U.S. multinationals. So maybe a correction such as the one that occurred on October 27 was meant to be. If so, my concern now is that we may be shrugging it off a little too quickly.

The day after the big 554-point drop, we received lots of calls from clients, as we did the day after the October 1987 crash, the biggest point drop in history. However, this year's calls had a very different tone than the 1987 calls. In '87, clients were very nervous and were asking if they shouldn't "jump ship" and take their losses. Very few, if any, wanted to rush in and buy at those much lower levels. This year the calls were almost entirely from clients asking what to buy and wanting to place a trade that very day. My initial thought was that folks are certainly more educated than they used to be; they understand the long-term nature of stock market investing, and instead of panicking about their current holdings going down, they want to put even more money to work at these now lower prices. Then I had a different thought: if our clients had really been listening to my advice, any money they had in reserves that wasn't intended for emergencies or other short-term needs would have already been in their long-term portfolios. They were actually calling to get into this downward-trending market to make some quick bucks and were willing to risk their cash reserves to do it. After all, we've learned that stocks just don't stay down very long, right? Who could blame these investors for such assumptions? Even if they were in the market when it tanked in '87, their portfolio probably did fine if they just held on. However, what we can never forget is that once in a while the market takes a dip that turns into a "bear market" that can leave scars on a portfolio—scars that, believe it or not, last longer than a week or two, or even a year. Recall this summer's newsletter article "Why Buy Bonds," which recounted the market decline of 1973 and 1974.

So what's my point? Am I predicting a bear market in the foreseeable future? Certainly not. I don't make near-term market predictions. In fact, I believe the stock markets of the world will continue to offer patient investors great potential for long-term returns. I also believe, however, that the old law "the higher the potential return, the higher the near-term risk" will never be repealed.

History suggests that sticking to a long-term, balanced approach—mixing the stocks of U.S. companies, non-U.S. companies, large companies, small companies, etc.—and riding through the inevitable ups and downs is how we stand the greatest chance of beating inflation and reaching our long-term financial goals.

Q&A—The Asian flu (currency crisis)

Q. I've heard a lot about the Asian crisis, but I'm not sure I understand what's really going on. Can you offer an explanation?

A. Let's look at Thailand. The Thai economy had an incredible run for ten years, beginning in 1987 when the Thai baht was pegged to move with our U.S. dollar. The Thai economy tripled in size between 1988 and 1996. Foreign investors literally forced money into Thailand. Credit was simply too cheap to resist, and, as you can imagine, too much debt led to financial disaster when the economy began to slow. The Thai stock market has lost half its value since its peak in 1993. Borrowers began struggling with their debt loads. And the overpriced property market burst and threatened to take the country's financial system with it.

Suddenly, Thailand seemed a very risky place to lend money, and the country's currency was dropping fast. Not only did foreigners stop throwing money at Thailand, they began pulling it out. The Thai government spent $23.4 billion in an attempt to defend their currency and another $12 billion propping up failing banks, but devaluation of the Thai currency was inevitable. There was suddenly 35% less money to repay foreign loans, compensate foreign investors, or purchase imported goods, services, and raw materials. Some estimates suggest that as many as one in ten Thai workers could lose their jobs.

As terrifying as all this sounds, it is certainly not unprecedented among our world's emerging nations. In 1994, Mexico received a multi-billion-dollar bail-out from the International Monetary Fund, which it has since paid back with interest. For Thailand, a $17 billion bail-out has been organized, with Japan making the largest contribution. It appears that any racing economy eventually has to downshift.

On the brighter side, the longer-term outlook for Thailand and the rest of Asia may not be as gloomy as it seems.

Thailand remains attractive in both its domestic market of sixty million consumers and its strategic location. The country is a gateway to the other emerging nations of Southeast Asia. Therefore, despite the current slowdown, Thailand still offers substantial opportunities to U.S. firms.

As for China, Hong Kong seems to be the current engine driving the economy, and if the first four months of unification are any indicator, China seems very content allowing Hong Kong to continue on its current path. Factor in China's huge population and current pace of industrialization, and you have a recipe for sustained growth well into the future.

So what should you, the smart investor, do now? Perhaps pony up as much cash as possible and buy a mutual fund concentrated in Asia? My response would be not to do anything dramatically different than you are currently, assuming your long-term portfolio is well-balanced and your allocation to non-U.S. stocks has some Asian exposure. If its time for rebalancing, you may want to consider repositioning some of your current long-term assets into these now lower-priced stocks of the world. But remember, foreign investments are subject to additional risks, such as the effects of ever-fluctuating exchange rates, foreign taxes, and volatile economic conditions.

"Patience, the Secret to Investment Success" was written mid-year 1998. At that point, the bull market had stretched beyond just about any historical reference point. Once again, in the article I expressed the view that market timing is a losing proposition. As illustrated in this book's foreword, a study performed by Dalbar Inc. suggests that the average equity investor earned a mere 3.90% annually from 1985 through 2004, while the S&P 500 Stock Index gained 11.90% per year. All the average Joe had to do was simply buy a diversified basket of stocks and hang on. But unfortunately, he acted on emotion, buying high, when seemingly everyone was making money, and selling low, when the going got tough.

Patience, the Secret to Investment Success
June 1998

These past ten years, according to Ibbotson Associates of Chicago, have been the best ten years in the history of the stock market. You would think that anyone in the market at all during this time period certainly made some nice money. While this is probably true for most, there are always those individual investors who just can't seem to ever make money in the stock market. Who are they? They may be the ones who got burned in '87 or '90 or '94, years when they may have just tested the water at the wrong time and watched their investment drop swiftly and very painfully. They quickly got out, vowing to never fish that pond again. And why did they cast their lines in the first place? Because they got tired of hearing their neighbor, best friend, poker buddy, barber, coworker, and countless others tell tales of profits made by investing in their favorite software company or growth mutual fund. They waited till they just couldn't bear it any longer and finally gave it a try. The market tanked, and their fears found all the justification they needed.

Now here we are, halfway through what could be the fourth up-double-digit year in a row for U.S. stocks. And here come the water-testers. My phone is ringing much more often these days with calls from friends and colleagues of clients who want to get in on some of those gains they've been hearing about for so long now.

Does this phenomenon spell the end for the long bull market? Who knows? Not me, I'm sorry to say. So am I scheduling meetings and helping these new clients invest their wealth? You bet. Are we just blindly throwing money into the market and expecting it to grow at the incredible pace many people have experienced? Nope, we're not. We're taking our time and having long talks and looks back to some of the bear markets of the past, like the two-year disaster of 1973 and '74. We're gaining an understanding that stock market investing has to be a long-term commitment, and we have to adhere to a reasonable strategy for making current and future decisions. We always diversify our clients' portfolios, and in many cases we're investing at least some money in, believe it or not, bonds.

As you read in last year's "Why Buy Bonds" article, history suggests that, at times, the returns on bonds may offset declining stock prices (however, past performance is no guarantee of future results). We're also investing overseas. There's no guarantee that history will repeat itself, but there is evidence that foreign investing can provide a stock portfolio not only with potential for substantial returns, but—in the right quantity—a possible hedge against downturns in the U.S. market. However, I believe that in a major market decline we will see sympathetic drops in markets around the world. It's in the aftermath that the truly healthy and reasonably priced markets will regain their positive momentum.

So what's the bottom line? If you have a long-term objective, buy long-term stuff, like stocks. Pick a sound strategy, and above all stick with it, especially when it's scary.

Here's yet another reminder that timing the market, quite frankly, almost never works. This article touches on the surprise reaction to the volatility of the '90s by 401(k) participants, illustrates the results of an analysis I performed with the help of CDA Weisenberger's "wrapper" mutual fund hypothetical software, and highlights a fascinating study that tracks the results of the market timing "experts" who, through their newsletters, make a living advising investors on when to buy and sell stocks. Of course, this begs the question, if a person truly knew precisely when to buy and sell stocks, why would that person ever need to sell a newsletter subscription?

One additional note: knowing that shifts in market direction can come without warning, the following is a tidbit for anyone out there still thinking that short-term timing or reacting to short-term market moves is worth considering:

- *$1 invested in the S&P 500 Stock Index in January 1926 would be worth $1,776.37 today. If you missed the one best month each year (perhaps by jumping out when it got scary and missing the rebound), that $1 would be worth $2.83 today[1] --- believe it or not.*

Timing the Stock Market
October 1998

A 1996 *Wall Street Journal* issue featured an article titled "Market Bumps Rattle Nerves at 401(k)s."[2] The article cited a study performed by human resources consultant Hewitt Associates LLP, which looked at fund trading in employee retirement plans at 25 large corporations.

According to the study, during a seven-day period in July 1996, the amount of money moving in and out of mutual funds by investors in some 401(k) plans increased by as much as six times the usual pace. This study's findings contradicted the widely held notion that 401(k) investors are passive and tend to hold their stock funds through rough times. I suspect the increased movements had to do with automation.

---

1 Dimensional Returns Program, CEG Worldwide analysis
2 Wall Street Journal, Market Bumps Rattle Nerves at 401(k)s, Hewitt Associates, August 23, 1996, C1

By and large, today's 401(k) plans allow participants to phone in and make investment changes at any time with the touch of a button. In the past, a participant was fortunate to have the ability to move on a quarterly basis.

The question being: is the wherewithal to quickly move in and out of the market ultimately a good thing for your everyday 401(k) participant? I'd say not necessarily, particularly when we consider the following hypothetical analysis and a recent study aimed at comparing market timing strategies to just buying and holding a diversified portfolio of stocks.

For starters, using CDA Weisenberger's "Wrapper" hypothetical software, let's compare two (Investor A and Investor B) very different investor personalities. Both invested $10,000 into an S&P 500 index fund on August 1, 1987, the month the bull market peaked, and added $100 per month going forward. Investor A stayed the course throughout the short but steep 1987 bear market (late August through early December), suffering a 33% hit to his portfolio.

Investor B jumped out of the market after the S&P dropped 10% and bought T-Bills, which, unlike mutual funds, offer government guarantees and fixed returns. B avoided the remaining 23% dip and waited patiently until July 1989, when the S&P 500 recovered to its pre–October '87 level.

Though A suffered a greater initial decline, his portfolio ultimately outperformed B's. By the time the S&P 500 recovered to its pre-crash level, A was ahead by more than $3,000. And by January 1996, A's portfolio totaled a handsome $46,203, while B's was worth $7,000+ less, with $38,877.

The best case scenario, of course, would've been to exit the market at the top and re-enter near the bottom (which is about as easy as hitting a million dollar jackpot in Vegas).

It's not unusual for a client to ask me if we shouldn't try to time the market, particularly after a month like July when stocks showed extreme volatility. This question assumes a mere mortal investment professional might accurately predict the future. And believe it or not, there are "experts" who, with their timing newsletters, make their living advising investors on when to get in and when to get out of stocks.

A 1994 study published in the Hulbert Financial Digest[3] tracked the performance of 108 market timing and economic forecasting newsletters for the previous five years. The findings were of no big surprise to asset allocation advocates like yours truly. Over the five-year period, only two of the newsletters studied came anywhere near predicting the actual results for the market and the economy. Offering virtually no hope for the individual investor thinking he can time the market while holding down a job and raising a family. I mean if experienced pros can't do it , odds are the individual investor can't either.

As I preach ad nauseam, the secret to long-term investment success is to establish the right mix of assets, rebalance to that mix periodically, make adjustments as your circumstances change, and never ever panic when the market's down.

---

3 Hulbert Financial Digest, Study of Market Timing & Economic Forecasting Newsletters, January 1994

At the risk of contradicting myself, seven years after writing "Why Buy Bonds", I wrote the following, "Beware the Bond." At the time (Spring 2004) bonds were rallying, and individual investors, tending to chase what's hot, were loading up. The debt market had just scored four consecutive years of positive results, and, unnoticed by return-hungry buyers, the factors that led to this extended rally no longer existed. My goal therefore was to simply tone down expectations for bonds going forward. I didn't suggest that investors should abandon their fixed income allocation altogether, but maybe shorten their maturities (less interest rate sensitive) and convert a bit to cash for the time being. Sure enough, at present, the luster seems to have left the bond market. According to Morningstar Mutual Funds, after an impressive four-year run (+9.38% in 2000, +10.40% in 2001, +10.52% in 2002, and +7.70% in 2003), the Lehman Brothers Credit Bond Index has experienced noticeably lower results since (+5.23% in 2004, and a barely positive 1.95% in 2005).

Beware the Bond
May 2004

Four years ago, investment advisers had a tough time convincing clients they should own bonds as part of a diversified portfolio. That's all changed with the bursting of the tech bubble and a three-year free fall in equities. While stocks crumbled, bonds blossomed, proving they can be a safe port in a storm. And today the bond, to the unsuspecting individual investor, looks as appealing as ever. With savings accounts, CDs, and money market funds paying a paltry 1%, a 3–6% yield on a corporate bond or bond fund is virtually irresistible.

So why not cash in the passbook account and buy the bond fund when you can make four times the interest? In a word, risk! What the yield-hungry investor perhaps doesn't understand is that bonds carry a great deal of interest rate risk; when rates drop, as they have of late, the price of existing bonds (possessing higher yields than newly issued bonds) typically increase. When rates rise however, making brand new bonds more attractive, the price of existing bonds tends to drop. So then, with interest rates at four-decade lows, an improving economy, and record budget deficits to finance, where do you think interest rates are headed? Ever-lower, or turning higher going forward? I'd be in the turning higher camp. And if I'm right, bond prices will suffer, disappointing the innocent soul who just couldn't take that low passbook rate any longer.

Now, I'm not suggesting that you completely abandon the bond component of your diversified long-term portfolio. I am suggesting, however, that you not let your frustration with low savings rates get the best of you. So what then do you with that CD or money market money earning 1%? If it's your emergency fund, keep it there. If it's part of your long-term portfolio, keep it there - for now. You may have an opportunity to buy bonds at a cheaper price in the not-too-distant future.

"But what about stocks?" You ask. "In the past twelve months the stock market has seen an amazing rebound. Shouldn't I rotate that bond money into the stock market?" Well, perhaps—but if, and only if, gaining more exposure to equities is consistent with your time horizon and temperament. It's too easy to lose our heads when it comes to our money. And generally, alas, when we lose our heads, we lose our money. In the '90s we experienced a bull market the likes of which we'd never seen. Unfortunately, the ensuing three-year decline was an experience not seen since the Great Depression. Many an unsuspecting investor got mesmerized by monster gains, only to suffer untold losses as the market crumbled in the early 2000s.

I'll never advocate trying to time the stock market; I'm forever a long-term buy and holder. Conventional wisdom suggests we allocate only that long-term portion (retirement plans for example) to the stock market. With target percentages to subclasses, such as large cap, small cap, international, and so on. Then, as our holdings fluctuate in value, we periodically rebalance back to our targets, maintaining our desired level of risk. That said, when it comes to the bond market, in an environment where the economy is growing and interest rates are coming off 40-year lows, a little market timing (meaning sidestepping mid- and long-term bonds for now) may be in order.

In "Market Direction," I expose my cynicism toward much of what you might call "retail" economic commentary. It's the kind of commentary that, candidly, I believe desperately attempts to paint an economic picture that is consistent with the political bias of the author (be he or she conservative or liberal). In reality, the economy is cyclical, with inevitable periods of expansion and contraction. Some politicians will experience the good fortunate of holding office during the growth phases of future cycles, while others will have the misfortune of presiding over the inevitable recessions to come. Make no mistake, no single office in the land, including the highest, has the power to materially impact the cyclical nature of the planet's largest economy.

Market Direction????
September 22, 2004

Many commentators, myself included, have characterized this year's stock market as lacking direction. After a very positive 2003, the market started out strong, only to give back the gains, and then some, by mid year. And now we're back in positive territory (just barely). So is the market truly directionless, or is the direction simply sideways? Is this a pause in a new bull market, or is it the calm before the next hurricane unleashes its fury on Wall Street? And can we possibly know for sure? One might think we could gain perspective by looking at the consensus among the nation's leading economists. But what consensus? Apparently, economists are a bit like politicians; they are as polarized today as Democrats and Republicans six weeks prior to a presidential election.

For example, I just recently read two distinctly different views on the economy in the same business periodical. The first article portrayed the current recovery from the 2001 recession as being "remarkably weak," stating that job growth has been the slowest of any recovery since the Great Depression and that the 2001 and 2003 tax cuts have accounted for only half of the 2004 budget deficit, and so on. What I expected to read in the end, but didn't, was that the current recovery has faced a few unusual challenges, not the least of which occurred on 9/11/2001. The article did not acknowledge that slower job growth this time around is largely due to gains in productivity (thanks to advances in technology, companies are much more efficient today compared to any past recovery); this year, in spite of record high oil prices and increased business caution, the numbers have picked up substantially with well over a million new jobs created year to date.

I then flipped to the second article, which presented a noticeably different view of our current state of affairs. The author of article number two painted a picture of very healthy economic growth. This article provided evidence that the industrial sector is rebounding—that growth in manufacturing is now at a par with the rapid pace of growth experienced in the late 1990s. The article further held that continued historically low interest rates (the Fed raising rates at merely a "measured" pace going forward) and benign inflation will continue to have positive effects on our economy into the foreseeable future. What I didn't see in article two were the negative statistics quoted in article one.

So whom do you believe: the pessimists, who don't seem willing to consider today's atypical circumstances, or the optimists, who would like us to believe that everything's peaches and cream? I'll say neither! I have a sneaking suspicion that if the political tables were turned, I'd read virtually the same articles, only the authors would be in opposite positions. Reality is likely somewhere in between.

Now back to the direction of the stock market. What's most striking to me today is the fact that stocks are up, at all, on a year-to-date basis. So much of the news these past few weeks has been negative: record-high oil prices, turmoil in Iraq, hurricanes pounding the Gulf Coast, uncertainty over the coming election, and corporate earnings not hitting expectations for several major U.S. companies. In spite of all this, the market has trended higher. Is it trying to tell us something? Is it just hanging in there, waiting for a little good news to send it to new heights? Or will it finally give way under the weight of all this uncertainty? In the short run, no one knows for sure. But in the long run, we can take comfort in the lessons of history. Our economy has seen much worse and prevailed—and there's no doubt in my mind that it will prevail once again. The U.S. stock market has been a very good investment for long-term investors with the proper perspective. Long-term investors understand that short-term volatility has been, and always will be, something they will have to accept in order to reap long-term rewards.

So my advice is to first make sure the only money you devote to stocks is your long-term money. Understand where you want to be financially in the future (in other words, establish your short- and long-term goals). Invest more when appropriate. Then check yourself to make sure you have the stomach to hang in there when things get choppy (if you don't, it's perfectly OK: you shouldn't lose sleep over your portfolio). And diversify; make sure you spread your portfolio among several different sectors of the economy. Follow these simple rules, and you stand a very good chance of reaching your goals. In the meantime, during this election year, take any economic forecast you come across with a grain of salt.

It's ironic that, when the sentiment surveys suggest the consumer is feeling very glum about the future, the stock market tends to rally. "When Bad News Is Good News" offers some statistical evidence that supports this notion plus theorizes as to why. Yet another example of how our instincts don't necessarily serve us well when it comes to making investment decisions.

When Bad News Is Good News
January 21, 2005

When is bad news good news for the stock market? It's when the surveys measuring investor sentiment tell us that the majority of investors, and the "experts" who advise them, are generally pessimistic on the stock market. That's right—when everyone's down, the market often goes up. Case in point: just before the current bull market began, the spring of 2003, only 40% of investors and 50% of investment newsletter writers were feeling good about stocks, according to the January 21, 2005 issue of *USA Today*[1]. And guess what, the Standard and Poor's 500 Index rose 26.4% that year and another 9% in 2004. Conversely, when the vast majority of the aforementioned folks are optimistic, look out! History suggests that major optimism tends to precede market pullbacks. And sure enough, the stock market has begun 2005 in miserable fashion, while, just three short weeks ago, optimism was rampant - with 60% of investors and 62% of the newsletter writers bullish. That's the highest since just before the 1987 crash. Now that's scary!

But not to worry, for I have good news—in just the past three weeks, the number of bullish investors has plummeted to 34%. They cite the Fed's inflation warnings and weaker-than-expected earnings by a few key companies as reasons for the sudden pessimism. Boy, what a relief! This may turn out to be a decent year after all.

I know it seems crazy on the surface, but the logic is sound. When investors are bullish, they tend to be fully invested—leaving little or no reserve cash to push the market higher. The only move they can make is to sell the minute a little bad news hits the press (Fed warnings, disappointing earnings, etc.). When investors are bearish, they tend to stay very liquid. They've already sold, so their next move can only be to put their cash back to work when things start looking up.

We know that volatility is a stock market reality. And one month's—or even one year's—results should not make or break a long-term investment strategy. Successful investors stay focused on the long-term and never panic when the near-term gets cloudy. And of course the near term is nothing but cloudy. We're in a brand new year, but we suffer the same old (2004) worries. Oil prices are rising, the Fed's raising interest rates, turmoil in the middle-east, the dollar's weak, etc. However, there are a few bright spots worth noting. The Fed's "beige book," an anecdotal survey of economic conditions in the twelve Federal Reserve Bank regions, released January 19, tells a story of solid business activity and steady consumer spending. Broadway ticket sales are breaking records, Florida theme parks are full, home sales have remained strong and business spending is expected to increase this year. And no more "jobless recovery"—our economy produced a respectable 2.2 million new jobs last year.

So with all this to ponder, one thing's for sure: 2005 will prove to be very interesting, and, I suspect, very volatile.

The stock market is a fickle thing. It climbs the highest peak one day, only to, with just the slightest breeze, fall off a cliff the next. And while fickleness is not your admirable trait, the following suggests that it is precisely what makes the stock markets of the world work.

Uncertainty—The Investor's Best Friend
August 2005

I can't believe we're already into the second half of the year. As they say, life is like a roll of toilet paper; the closer we get to the end, the faster it goes. I just read the letter I wrote this time last year, and, to quote Yogi Berra, "it's like déjà vu all over again." Last July, the Fed was raising short-term interest rates, oil was up sharply, stocks were flat, and uncertainty prevailed. And here we sit a year later, the Fed just raised rates yet again, oil just reached an all-time high, the major stock indexes are barely positive on the year, and yes, indeed, the outlook is nothing but murky.

But come to think of it, as long as I've been paying attention, I can't remember a time when the outlook wasn't at least somewhat cloudy. And, quite frankly, I wouldn't have it any other way. The fact is, the "market" couldn't exist in a world of certainty, i.e., if anyone truly figured it out (it'll never happen), the ball game's over. You see, for the stock market to function, for every eager buyer there must exist a willing seller. In other words, there has to be an opposition to every opinion regarding every security offered on every organized exchange. Otherwise, there would be no transactions and therefore no opportunity. As strange as it may seem, short-term uncertainty is exactly what we need in order to benefit from the long-term opportunity stocks can offer.

Yes, I know, you skeptic—it's different today; the world is different, less certain than ever, more volatile! We can't consider history; the world today is so different than anything we've faced thus far.

Well my friend, I beg to differ. Of course the world has seen its share of uncertainty over the last hundred years: the Great Depression, two world wars, periods of deflation and hyper inflation, the Cold War, currency crises, a 90% tax rate on dividends and interest,

Vietnam, OPEC, two impeachments, 9/11, Iraq, the Internet bubble burst, ten extended bear markets (periods where stocks declined 20% or more), and so on. In spite of it all, the market has consistently delivered for the long-term, patient investor. The key is patience and, at times, a strong stomach. I.e., to be successful, we must survive the down markets—which, by the way, are inevitable and absolutely essential for the market to work long-term. The down markets keep the uncertainty, and therefore the opportunity, alive.

I'm making no prediction here. I can't tell you where the market will be one year from now. But I'm very comfortable with its prospects over the next ten or fifteen.

With that in mind, I'll close with the basic tenets of our investment philosophy:

- The design of the portfolio as a whole is more important than the selection of any particular security within the portfolio. The appropriate allocation of capital among asset classes (stocks, bonds, cash, etc.) will have far more influence on the long-term portfolio results than the selection of individual securities. Investing for the long-term (preferably longer than ten years) becomes critical to investment success, as it allows the long-term characteristics of an asset class to surface.
- Diversification can help reduce investment volatility. The proportional mix of asset classes determines long-term risk and return characteristics of the portfolio as a whole.
- Portfolio risk can be decreased by increasing diversification and by lowering the correlation of market behavior among the asset classes selected. (Correlation is the statistical term for the extent to which two asset classes move in tandem or opposition to each other.)
- Investing globally can help to minimize overall portfolio risk due to the imperfect correlation between the economies of the world. Investing globally has also been shown historically to enhance portfolio returns,

although there is no guarantee that it will do so in the future.

- Equities offer the potential for higher long-term investment returns than cash or fixed income investments. Equities also possess more volatility. Investors seeking higher rates of return should consider increasing the proportion of equities in their portfolio while at the same time accepting a greater variation in results (including occasional declines in value).
- Picking individual equity securities and timing the purchasing or sale of investments in an attempt to "beat the market" are highly unlikely to improve long-term investment results. In fact, such activity is likely to significantly increase overall risk, and, therefore, with few exceptions, such practices are to be avoided.

One of the most frustrating events to witness, personally speaking, is when the chairman of the Federal Open Market Committee (FOMC), now Ben Bernanke, sits before a group of elected officials (usually the United States Congress), many of whom have very little understanding of the cyclical nature of our economy and the role of the FOMC (as evidenced by the nature of their questions). He delivers a statement, then answers questions (which are often preceded by intense criticism of the FOMC) regarding current interest rate policy. In my opinion, this is an egregious waste of time and taxpayer money. The Fed should be left alone to do its work and should never even consider the politically motivated rants and pleas from these distinguished ladies and gentlemen. I want the Fed governors to do only what they feel is right, regardless of how anyone (particularly a politician) may feel about how the Fed's decisions might impact the economy in the short run. Like the economy, the stock market moves in a cyclical fashion and will ultimately reflect the realities of the business world. Sure, it would be nice to make money in stocks year after year, but no matter how bad we may want it, it ain't happening. And, quite frankly, it shouldn't. Trust me; we want the market to accurately reflect the present business environment. Read on, and you'll understand what I mean.

Nine Thousand or Twelve Thousand?
January 2006

Nine thousand or twelve thousand? Where will the market end 2006? This question was recently posed to a panel of experts on a program aired by a popular financial television network. I'm sorry to disappoint, but I'm not telling how the experts answered. Quite frankly, it doesn't matter, and their responses will have no measurable, long-term impact on the portfolio of the wise, long-term investor. I may have an opinion on where the market is headed in the short run, but my one true hope is that it does precisely what it should in light of how economic events unfold over the course of the year.

You see, when the economy slows and businesses suffer, stock prices ultimately need to fall, accurately reflecting the true value of the underlying companies. When the economy moves ahead at a healthy (yet non-inflationary) pace, stocks will ultimately rise, reflecting an improving business environment.

Let us never forget what can occur when the market fashions together a bull run that extends beyond what corporate and economic reality would suggest. We all saw the Internet bubble burst in early 2000, catching many unsuspecting, tech-crazed investors off guard. Following a huge run-up in stocks in the late nineties that took the market to heights the underlying fundamentals couldn't justify, a bear market developed (2000 through 2002), the likes of which our country hadn't seen in over seventy years. But in the end, the only investors who actually suffered unrecoverable losses were those who panicked and sold while the market fell, as well as the tech-crazed who loaded their portfolios with Internet companies, the names of which I can't recall. The well-diversified, long-term thinkers who only sell when it's time to spend some money likely fared just fine. It's not that they didn't see their portfolios decline on paper (believe me, they did), it's that they simply refused to follow the herd and sell when things got scary. Wise long-term investors know that the economy and the markets move in cycles, and if they are not in current need of their money (or more than their usual monthly distribution), they believe they'll be just fine in the long run. Some were even so bold as to increase their (well-diversified) positions of fundamentally sound companies (or the mutual funds buying these companies) when the rest of the world was selling in a blind panic.

So if the market goes to twelve thousand next year due to solid fundamentals and a good economy, I'm all for it. If the market drops to nine thousand because of a slowing business environment and weakening economy, I'm all for it. If, when you retire, the equity portion of your portfolio provides results consistent with the market's long-term average return, you simply shouldn't care what it does between now and then. If you get too excited about the short term (less than ten years), you run the risk of getting caught up in the moment—either buying too much of a hot sector or selling in a down market. In either case, the results can be devastating. We can not control the market's behavior, but we can certainly control our own. Or, in other words, the market's behavior may determine our short-term investment success, but in the long term (when it counts), our success will be in direct proportion to how well we behaved along the way.

SECTION TWO

Bear Markets

In January 1995, investors were licking surface wounds suffered from what I'd call the mini–bear market of 1994 (the S&P 500 and the NASDAQ Composite Indexes ended '94 just slightly off from where they began the year). In "Keep a Long-Term Perspective," I caution the equity investor not to give in to the urge to sell when the market takes a dip. As it turns out, 1995 saw a huge turnaround in the broad market, rewarding those who hung in there.

Keep a Long-term Perspective
January 1995

Talk to any financial professional these days about your investments, and you will probably be told to keep a long-term perspective. If you just bought your first growth mutual fund in January of last year, because you couldn't let that CD reinvest at 3.5% (the average 1 year rate in January 1994), you might be wondering if you didn't just make a big mistake. After paying that 5% sales load and watching the share price of your fund dip further and further after you made this treacherous decision, you realize that if you cashed in today, you would receive less, a lot less than you invested. All of a sudden, that 3.5% CD with its guaranteed return of principal looks pretty good, especially now that it's paying 5.5%.

What's worse is that no one knows for sure when (or if) your fund will get back to even, allowing you to escape with your original investment. Chalking the whole thing up to experience, you vow to never again venture beyond investments that are insured by the U.S. government.

Given Wall Street's myopia, it's no wonder investors tend to focus on the short-term dynamics of our economy and to ignore the enduring reality that true investing is a long-term proposition.

If you bought your growth mutual fund with a long-term perspective, your biggest mistake would probably be to sell if or when your account breaks even. While there are no guarantees, history has proved that patient investors who buy stocks in a diversified fashion need simply to remain patient. Consider these statistics compiled by Ibbotson Associates of Chicago.[1]

- The S&P 500 index has grown an average of roughly 10% per year for the past 66 years. Money funds and cash equivalents (T-Bills, short-term CDs, etc.) have returned an average of approximately 3.7% per year for the same time period.
- Equity investments are more volatile than money funds and cash equivalents. Timely payment of principal and interest is guaranteed for T-Bills, and CDs. While stocks offer no such guarantee, it is worth noting that over 10-year holding periods, the S&P 500 index has increased in value 96% of the time.
- An investment in the S&P 500 for the period of 1980 to 1989 would have realized an annual 17.50% rate of return. If the investor happened to miss the ten best performing days, perhaps by attempting to time the market, his or her average return would have fallen to 12.60% annually. Past performance is no indication of the future; however, history suggests that, other than rebalancing periodically, your target mix of stocks, bonds, etc., should only be altered when your objectives change or when you are nearing a goal, such as retirement or college education, not when you think the market has peaked. To date, not one published study exists that proves the so-called "market timers" can consistently beat the market.

---

1 Ibbotson Associates "Stocks, Bonds, Bills and Inflation" 1994 Edition

In July 2000, the bear market was just beginning to gain momentum. The following article illustrates the benefits of reducing volatility through diversification. As it turned out (considering the bear market to come), this was a very timely message.

Managing Risk—Protect the Downside
July 2000

John is an aggressive investor and proud of it. He's been investing in the stock market for three and a half years and has been weighting his portfolio heavily to a few high-flying technology stock funds. His strategy is to concentrate his portfolio in the hottest sector and get rich as fast as he can. He's had some winners and some losers, but overall he was quite proud of his three-year average return of 20% up to this January. In fact, he's still proud of his accomplishment even though his portfolio has dropped 20% during the past six months. Who can complain, after making 20% for three years; one 20% drop isn't the end of the world. Overall he's still doing great, certainly much better than those scaredy-cats who can't stand the heat and drag down their returns by diversifying into other areas in an attempt to lower risk, right?

Well, let's take a look at the results achieved by one of these scaredy-cats, whom we'll call Jane. Jane considers herself a moderate risk taker. She believes that investing in stocks over the long run is right for her but isn't comfortable putting everything into just one sector of the economy. Therefore she invests across a broader range of sectors, including health care, financials, and several others, as well as technology. She even allocates 25% of her portfolio to the stocks of companies based outside the U.S. For the three years ending January 1, she didn't do quite as well as John. Her average return was a respectable 15%, which doesn't stack up all that well against John's 20%. However, when we factor in the developments between January and July of this year, we make a startling discovery. Jane's portfolio did drop, but not by the 20% that John's suffered; her portfolio gave back just 5%. Although her technology stocks took a big hit, the other sectors held up well, particularly the health care sector, which experienced a great six months. Jane's current average annual return since she began is now 11.04%. And, believe it or not, that's considerably better than John's average of only 9.66% during the same period. Just one down year after three years of huge returns makes John's results look mediocre compared to the more conservative Jane's. The moral of this hypothetical story is, *if you go for broke, you just may get there, or, if you're really lucky, like our aggressive investor John, you might end up average.*

My concern at the moment is for the unsuspecting investor just now venturing into the market. It's been tough for this rookie investor, listening to friends constantly boast of how easy it's been to make huge, double-digit returns. The rookie finally jumps in, gets on the Internet, and begins investing his life savings into the three of the top-performing mutual funds in 1999. You can guess what happens next. The top funds were, of course, the ones weighted heavily, if not entirely, to technology stocks. And tragically, when the tech bubble began to burst, that rookie investor's life savings became a whole lot less in a very short period of time.

If you happen to be one of these newbies thinking about taking the plunge with your life savings, take my advice; if you have the stomach for volatility, by all means invest a portion of your long-term assets in stock funds, *but don't chase returns!* Instead, *diversify! Spread* your assets out, buy into several different sectors (even those areas that didn't do well last year), invest in mutual funds, and take advantage of the potential gains in the growing economies outside the U.S. by allocating a portion of your investments to international mutual funds. You may not hit a grand slam, but you'll greatly increase your odds of winning the ball game—in other words, meeting your long-term goals.

The next article, also written in July 2000, asks the question: if, assuming a relatively low rate of return, an investor is on track to accumulate capital sufficient to fulfill all his wants and needs, why would he expose any of his portfolio to the stock market?

Why Take the Risk?
July 2000

Pick up any financial publication, including many of my past newsletters, or listen to any of the "gurus" on CNBC, and you'll be advised that at virtually whatever stage of life you're in, you should invest a portion of your long-term portfolio in stocks—particularly if you're young and have twenty or more years to retirement. Fortyish investors would be advised to maintain a large portion, if not all, of their portfolios in the stock market. Conceptually, I am in complete agreement. History suggests that the longer your time frame, the higher your odds of seeing positive returns from equities.

I believe, however, that there are two more important factors investors must consider in determining how to allocate their retirement assets. The first is the investors' emotional wherewithal (or lack thereof) to withstand the inevitable volatility of the stock market, and the second is determining what rate of future return is actually necessary to attain the investors' retirement-income goal. We've touched on risk tolerance considerations in several past newsletters, so for this issue we'll focus on why it's not always necessary, from a rate of return standpoint, to take on the market's volatility. Let's consider a hypothetical scenario.

John and Jane Sample are both forty years old, they've done a good job saving for their two children's college education, and they are now focusing on planning for their own retirement. Over the past ten years they've accumulated $150,000 in 401(k) accounts and IRAs and currently contribute a total of $12,000 each year to their various plans. Additionally, Jane's employer provides a defined benefit pension plan from which she'll receive a monthly income at retirement. They recently hired a financial adviser to assist them in devising a plan to accumulate enough funds to retire comfortably in twenty years. After a fact-gathering session in which John and Jane communicated their goals to their adviser, she was able to make some projections into the future based on their current retirement assets, ongoing retirement plan contributions, and a projected future annual inflation rate of 4%. As it turns out, John and Jane are doing just fine. In fact, if they can earn a before-tax average annual return of 7.2% on their portfolio for the next twenty years, they should be able to reach all of their retirement goals. Now that they have a clear picture of where they're going, it's time for the Samples to adopt an investment strategy for the next twenty years.

As mentioned in the first sentence, based on their age and years to retirement, conventional wisdom would suggest a heavy allocation to stocks. However, one could argue that it's not at all necessary for the Samples to take on any market risk whatsoever. If all they need is 7.2% per year (which we could almost get today in one-year CDs), why indeed would they want to take on the risk of the stock market? Of course, interest rates could trend lower over time (well below the 7.2% needed), inflation could increase above the projected rate, or they may have underestimated what they'll actually need at retirement. Any one of these factors would make achieving their goal impossible unless they earn a higher return, save more money, or both. But all in all, based on today's projections, they really don't need to take on a lot of risk.

However, there's a good chance they will anyway, at least to some extent. And who could blame them? The case for sustained growth in the technology-driven economies around the world is compelling. Not many people want to miss out on what could be many more years of exceptional growth in equities. That said, I firmly believe that couples like the Samples who simply don't need to stretch for higher returns should invest prudently and cautiously, perhaps allocating a reasonable percentage to equities to protect against inflation but not overexposing themselves to any one sector of the economy or to stocks in general.

Going through the process of identifying your retirement needs and objectives, then projecting the necessary savings rate and rate of investment return needed to get there will help you determine the degree of risk you'll need to accept for your portfolio. If you're already retired and have adequate income sources, stocks or stock mutual funds, in moderation, can still play an important roll in your portfolio as a potential way to keep up with inflation. The key word here is *moderation.*

"Here We Go Again" was written just seven months into the huge bear market that lasted all the way to March 2003. Like so many of my newsletters, this one was designed to calm investors' nerves and keep them thinking long-term. As you read on, you may get a sense that I wasn't the least bit concerned about the level of downward volatility we had seen to that point. The tone might have been a bit more cautionary had I known what was in store. However, I did warn in the end that bear markets will come, I just didn't realize at the time that the next one had already begun.

Here We Go Again!
October 2000

It's Thursday, October 12, 2000, and it's days like this that truly inspire me to write this newsletter. The Dow Jones Industrial Average ended down nearly 400 points today, and the NASDAQ Composite Index was off nearly 100. It's amazing to me how well just about all of you (those of you readers whom we counsel) seem to accept downward volatility these days. Back in the late '80s, this kind of volatility sparked multiple phone calls of a panicky nature, clients asking if it's time to jump ship and save what's left. Virtually no one wanted to buy stocks back then, while the market was falling. During this past, very scary week, with few exceptions, callers have been anxious to buy while things appear cheap.

Now, I know that many of you non-callers, to whom this newsletter is devoted, are worried but don't bother to call, because you already know what I'm going to say. And of course you're right; I will preach the virtue of long-term buy-and-hold investing as opposed to emotionally-driven market timing. During the past sixteen years of working with clients and studying the dynamics of investing, I have become a firm believer that the true secret to success in investing is patience and diversification. That doesn't mean you shouldn't have a little fun and devote a small portion of your portfolio to your favorite tech stock—just do it with an amount of money that won't disrupt your retirement plans if you lose it.

In a recent newsletter, we painted a picture of two hypothetical investors: one was the risk taker, the other the asset allocator. The asset allocator performed better over time, in spite of underperforming in up markets. The secret was to outperform in down markets by investing in a good mix of asset classes. Of course, even the portfolio with the diversified mix of assets is still going down on days like today. So what about today—is the sky really falling, or is this just another replay of the kinds of "corrections" we've been experiencing lately, where the market skyrockets to new highs shortly after a breathtaking drop? I wish I knew, but truly I don't—and, believe me, neither does anyone else. The "experts" on CNBC who predicted this drop (that would be two of the many guests on CNBC the past few months) were just very lucky. As many of you have heard from me, ad nauseam, the worst thing that can happen, in terms of market timing, is hit it right on the money the very *first* time. And why would that be the worst thing? Because you'll believe you can do it again, and you'd try, and you'd lose, big time..

So what about right now? The market's getting killed, and it feels like it'll last forever. Oil prices are going through the roof. The Euro's in the dumps. Third-quarter earnings are coming in lower than expected. The situation looks ugly, and for now it's hard to find the light at the end of the tunnel. And believe it or not, I'm not going to try and convince anyone that this is yet another near-term buying opportunity (we don't time the market, remember?). Instead, I'm taking you on a journey, into the future, with the hope that if you've been sweating the market lately, you'll sleep a little easier tonight.

First of all, if you have money in the stock market that you plan on spending in the near-future, it has no business being in the stock market. So I'm assuming that the money you're concerned about is part of your long-term portfolio.

There are two simple steps to a good night's sleep. Step one; think long-term. You've read in many past newsletters the statistics suggesting that long holding periods can substantially reduce the risk of the stock market.

Step two; observe your surroundings: When you drive to work tomorrow, keep your eyes on the road, but when it's safe, take a look around. You'll see other drivers on their way to work. Those drivers will collect their paycheck on Friday as they always do, with the usual deductions like Social Security, state and federal taxes, and their 401(k) contributions. They'll cash their check and spend a big portion on the kids this weekend at the big Fresno Fair. You'll also see their children getting on and off the school bus, or riding their Razor scooters at $89.95 each (I know this from personal experience), wearing their brand-new Nikes at a minimum of $50 a pair and new winter coats ranging from $35 to $80 apiece. And think about next year when those feet will be bigger and someone invents an even better scooter. Look at all those new SUVs the parents are driving. Aren't the new models cool? Next year's models will be even cooler, and trust me; people will be buying them next year too.

You see, these baby-boomers constitute the biggest generation in the history of our country. According to Harry S. Dent, author of the best seller *The Roaring 2000s*, the next eight to nine years will be the peak spending years for this huge generation of American citizens. Peak spending means peak profits and, consequently, higher stock prices. Not only will these boomers be spending, but they'll have to invest as well to continue to support their fabulous lifestyles well into their retirement years. Unfortunately, we don't hear this enough on CNBC; instead, we hear more about things like price to earnings ratios, oil prices, interest rates, and pro forma earnings growth. I do pay attention to these present-day statistics, mainly so I can sound smart when we do our quarterly and semi-annual reviews. Longer-term, it's spending patterns that count.

Essentially, what I'm saying is that if you're truly a long-term investor, I suggest you pay more attention to the world around you. If you see people spending money, and if you see more technological innovation where you work (important so companies can gain efficiencies to meet the demand), my guess is you'll be very happy with your long-term investment results, but only if you hang in there.

That said, in the final analysis, I have to say that nothing is worth losing sleep over. So if your fear during times like these affects your daily life, you need to reconsider your overall strategy. One thing I know for sure is that as good as the market may possibly be over the next few years, there will be many, many scary moments as we move higher. In essence, volatility—downward volatility—has been and always will be a fact of life for equity investors. History suggests that the investors who can put the blinders on during the tough times will be rewarded in the end.

"Stock Market Mentality" offers a very practical view of long-term equity investing. In February 2001 we were coming off a very negative 2000. The extent of the decline, particularly in many NASDAQ-traded stocks, took virtually everyone by surprise. This article was very timely, given what was happening, but the logic behind viewing your portfolio as property, rather than a bank account, is timeless.

Stock Market Mentality
February 2001

In the last issue I made the case for a bright long-term future for the equity markets, based on spending patterns and the huge baby boom population, even though we just endured the worst year in the history of the NASDAQ Index (down nearly 40% in 2000), a 9% drop in the Standard & Poor's 500 Index, and a 15% decline for the Europe, Australia, and Far East Index (according to BigCharts.com). If, as they say, adversity is our greatest teacher, where's the lesson in last year's bloodbath? As it turns out, there were several, but the most important was the emotional experience of living through a dramatic drop in stocks; the lesson was in self-knowledge. The question you should ask is: do I truly belong in the market? You get to the answer by asking yourself the following: Did I lose any sleep last year as my portfolio was dropping in value? Did I postpone my vacation plans? Did I spend less at Christmastime because I was worried about my portfolio? Did my spouse "rake me over the coals" about how our 401(k) plan was performing? If you answered "yes" to one or more of these questions, you have two choices:

1. Get out of the market altogether. Your long-term portfolio shouldn't make you miserable.

   OR

2. Change the way you think about your portfolio—in other words, gain a new perspective.

Let's focus for now on the second option, gaining a new perspective. You see, while growing up, only a few of us were given any insight into how investing works. We started our savings experience at our parents' bank. We made deposits to a savings account, and once a month we added the interest we earned to our balance. The only way that savings account could decline in value was if we made a withdrawal. With this introduction to investing, our natural reaction to a big drop in our retirement plan value is pure nausea. How could it be that I had a gazillion dollars in my retirement plan on January 1, added to it during the year, and now have a lot less than a gazillion dollars 12 months later? It feels as though someone stole the money right out of my bank account. That's the place we go instinctively; that's our perspective. The question then is, is this the proper perspective? The answer is "yes," but only if we sold our holdings after the decline in value. Once they're sold at a loss and the proceeds go to the bank account, we have truly lost the money. But perhaps more tragically, we have lost our investment, and that's what will hurt the most, considering the long-term nature of our retirement portfolios. Speaking for myself and my family, we are very much in the accumulation phase of our lives. My kids are young, I enjoy my work, and I don't expect to retire for another couple of decades. The money I'm investing now will not generate income for many years into the future. Therefore, my objective is to accumulate as much investment assets as I possibly can (I get more when the market goes down) now, so I can sell them, ideally, at much higher prices in the future.

To make my point, let's pretend for a moment that we're not investing in our retirement plans, but in real estate. Those of us living in or near Fresno know that for many years the growth in our area has been moving to the north. Let's say we believe that this will continue, and we have some money to invest that we won't need to touch for say 15 years. So we find a few acres far out to the north and make the investment. In addition, we plan to invest more money each year into the land surrounding our initial plot. In essence, for the next 15 years we're not going to sell a thing, only continue to accumulate. Therefore, what we really want to see happen, at least for the next several years, is not property values going up, but going down, way down, so we can buy lots of property really cheap. We hope to need wide-angle binoculars to see all the land we'll own 15 years from now. What the price does between now and then isn't the issue.

You see, the most successful long-term investors are only concerned with buying while they're young. If they have the proper perspective, they don't view down markets as negatives, but as huge positives—opportunities to buy more when things are cheap. The primary difference between this real estate analogy and our mutual fund or stock portfolio is that, via the Internet, we can get a free appraisal of our portfolio every minute of every weekday. To appraise our real estate, on the other hand, we have to hire a professional. Therefore, we're not likely to have the real estate appraised more often than every few years. Some of us are valuing our portfolios every few minutes. And therein lies the problem. If we constantly focus on the minute-to-minute dollar value of the portfolio, we're completely missing the fact that, in a declining market, the number of shares we own increases considerably—that is to say, we purchased more property at a cheaper price.

Now, if you aren't currently adding to your portfolio, you might say this scenario doesn't apply to you, when in reality it probably does—particularly if you've invested in growth mutual funds. Growth funds often distribute capital gains during the year that, if they aren't being used for income, get reinvested into the funds, thus buying more shares. When the fund's share price is down, you accumulate more shares.

This new perspective is fine and dandy as long as you can identify that your portfolio is down due to the overall movement in the financial markets, rather than down due to poor holdings. If the major market averages were up 10% for the year and your portfolio of equities was down 10%, this would not be a time to feel good about buying more. Such a case would indicate that something is definitely wrong with the portfolio, requiring your immediate attention. If, however, both the market and the growth portion of your portfolio are down, I think this perspective makes perfect sense. You just want to be sure that your overall performance is in line with the appropriate benchmarks.

So there you have it. If you buy into this "proper perspective," last year may have been a very important year for your portfolio, as you would have increased your holdings nicely while prices dropped, and you'll want to stick with your long-term strategy. If not, and if you know you'll worry when you experience the inevitable market declines, it may be time for you to rid yourself of the more volatile components of your portfolio.

It never ceases to amaze me how the stock market commentary of the past sounds so much like it could have been stated just yesterday. "Never Trust Your Instincts" was written right in the middle of the most recent bear market. The quotes from the past remind us that bear markets are nothing new and, as I express so often in this book, nothing that intelligent, long-term investors with well-diversified portfolios ever react to.

Never Trust Your Instincts (When it Comes to Investing)
September 2001

The bubble has burst. Following an unprecedented and unwarranted wave of euphoria, stock prices have tumbled, in particular for the NASDAQ technologies that led on the way up. As a result, investor confidence has taken a beating and mutual fund assets have declined. The mutual fund boom is definitely over. It may be years until funds gain their luster.

Sound familiar? This is what John Rekenthaler, research director at Morningstar Mutual Funds, says he was hearing when he first joined Morningstar as an associate fund editor in February 1988.

The U.S. economy will perk up again. Corporate earnings will improve and the stock market will recover. Why? Because we live in a free society and that leads to new development, new growth, jobs, and stock market appreciation. It's very difficult to think positively when the stock market falls almost daily and many are predicting a stagnant economy and a do-nothing stock market for years to come. If buying stocks at the right time were easy, everybody would be rich. It's hard to bring yourself to buy stocks when some market gurus are predicting the end of the world, or worse. If it's all over, you might as well go out a big stockholder. Excessive fears create excessive values but only for those who are willing to fight the mobs' emotions and get up to bat. Do not listen to the doom Sayers, do not listen to the crowd, do use common sense, do buy quality stocks when they get dumped to historically low levels in relation to their fundamentals, do be patient, do be one of the ones we call lucky six months to a year from now.

This is what Al Goldman, of A.G. Edwards, said in September 1990 when the Dow Jones Industrial Average was at 2,545. Since then we've seen a mild recession, the Gulf War, the Asian and Mexican currency crises, the Russian bond default, and the current bear market—and still the Dow sits around 10,000.

Nearly every man who makes an investment violates the principles he applies to his own business. Relying on merely a superficial knowledge of all that is involved, he undertakes to manage the entire job himself. Whether an investor or speculator he begins by buying at the tops and ends by selling at the bottoms. The various articles he reads in the newspaper about prosperity, bumper crops, shortage in freight cars, heavy foreign trade balances, factories running over-time inspire him with confidence. His own business booming, collections are good and the tight fisted bankers are using his dollars to make more dollars to their personal profit. Even the smug sum in the savings account drawing 3 to 4% interest points an accusing finger. Put me to work says Mr. Bank Balance, give me a chance to prove my metal, I too can grow like Jack's Bean Stalk, don't you know that Mr. Next Door Neighbor made X? Mr. Average Investor has heard enough, he buys something, anything; he follows the crowd and buys what everyone else is buying. When the inevitable reaction comes and the pendulum swings the other way, when demagogues stand on the graves of great dead industries and bolster the multitudes of the unemployed of their bloody deeds and prices crumble daily, the odds are fearful that Mr. Average Investor again follows the crowd and sells when everyone else is selling. He begins with a light heart and a heavy pocketbook and ends with a heavy heart and a light pocketbook. What has he gained? Experience. What is his conclusion? That the investment of money requires knowledge and experience in the same degree that the management of his own business requires specific knowledge and experience. That the times to invest, either for income or profit, are when good securities are selling near their average low prices and are thankful if they go lower that he may buy more at a cheaper price.

This quote, from Charles Merrill of Merrill Lynch, is every bit as relevant today as it was when he said it—in the year 1911.

Over the past 18 months, the stock market has seen a downward trend that virtually no one had anticipated. In fact, if you told me 12 months ago that the NASDAQ Composite Index would lose 50% of its value over the following year, I would have argued intelligently that given the state of the economy and corporate environment at the time, such a decline was highly unlikely. Nonetheless, here we are. Today the U.S. economy doesn't look good. Industrial production has declined steadily for nearly a year. Our manufacturing sector has not suffered this much since the 1991 recession, and the Labor Department just reported the largest productivity drop since 1993. So now what? With all this bad news, we might as well dump all our stock market holdings and vow never to go down that road again. But before we take that dramatic leap, let's look back at how the market has performed following the economic slowdowns of the past, as illustrated in the opening quotes, and then consider whether or not we should abandon ship.

Let's assume that we're not out of the woods yet, economically speaking. If indeed we are in a recession and it's only half over, let's see how the stock market has performed 18 months after the mid point of past recessions. According to the September 2001 issue of *Smart Money Magazine*, the average large-cap investment return, 18 months after the midpoint of all 13 recessions since 1926, was 34%. Small-cap returns were even better, averaging 40% to 50% for the year and a half following the midpoint of each recession.

Now for the stock market itself. I went back to 1973 and '74 in CDA Wiesenberger's database to see how the NASDAQ Composite Index performed after a bear market that saw losses like the ones just experienced by the NASDAQ of today. The index dropped a cumulative 53.80% during the bear market of '73 and '74. Then in 1975, by which time I'm sure it felt as though the world had come to an end, the NASDAQ shot higher by 32.89%. In 1976 the index was up 28.03%, and for the five years following the drop in '73 and '74 the NASDAQ gained an average annual return of 22.57%. And I assure you it felt just as ugly in 1974 as it does today.

The message from the past is clear: invest now in a well-diversified portfolio or, if you're already invested, stay invested in a well-diversified portfolio, and you may very well have solid gains by 2003. As always, the key is to stay diversified. Even if you're in the camp that believes the tech stocks of the NASDAQ will come bounding back next year, please do not mortgage your home to buy them. In fact, I would suggest you not over-weight any single sector but rather just be sure you have some exposure to growth stocks, some to value stocks (both large and small), some non-U.S. stocks, real estate, and perhaps some bonds to keep everything in balance. Your particular mix should be determined based upon your stage in life and your personality, never on what you might think will make you rich over the next twelve months.

"Don't Worry, Be Happy" was written in early 2002. At that point we had just experienced two consecutive years of stock market decline, a phenomenon very few of my clients had ever witnessed (the 1973–1974 bear market was the most recent two-year decline at that time). My purpose here was to explain the forces that led to the bear market and examine the two-year evolution of these factors. As it turned out, the bear market stretched to three years, and 2002 saw the biggest decline. In hindsight you could say that 2002 provided the wash-out needed to finally put an end to the extended decline. In other words, 2002 saw the darkness before the dawn. I believe it's imperative that every investor realize that bear markets are inevitable and understand that they ultimately serve a very important purpose: they remove the excesses that accumulate during virtually every extended bull market.

Don't Worry, Be Happy
February 2002

It's been a rough road these past two years, to say the least, especially for the stock market investor who had expectations of growing riches at the incredible pace seen in the '90s. It was worse yet for the investor who invested money that he or she actually needed to spend during the past two years. For the investor with high expectations, read on—you may gain a new perspective. For the investor needing the money, I hope you balanced your portfolio with a fair portion of bonds and can use that money while waiting for a recovery. If not, you've learned a valuable lesson: stock market investing (as opposed to trading) is meant only for those with long time horizons.

If you're the long-term investor, with time to wait, these past two years may prove to have been the most critical to your long-term success. I make this seemingly illogical statement for a couple of reasons. First of all, you've read many times before in this newsletter that you should buy more shares when the market is down, either through periodic investments or reinvestment of dividends and capital gains. Secondly, consider the energizing factor. Lewis J. Walker

CFP, in an enlightening article featured in the *Journal of Financial Planning* July 2001[1], writes:

> In early 2001, we were bombarded with the negative implications of the NASDAQ Index plunging 62% from its historical high of 5,048 on March 10, 2000. But ponder this: we have not had a 62% reduction in creativity, brain power, or entrepreneurial skills. A shakeout of a Richter scale eight-point magnitude compels companies and individuals to get creative, to refocus and become more competitive. An implosion in stock prices is a form of stabilization, forcing better economic policy, improved corporate governance and deliberative approaches to investment policy. The technology and talent that once led to the market's over-valuation is still there. The sober resolve to do it again is the promise of advancement.

Add to this the reality that the largest portion of the baby boomer population is entering the stage in life where personal consumption is generally at it's highest level (they spend lots of money), and you have the formula for increased corporate profits, leading to noticeably higher stock prices.

It helps during tough economic times like these to look back and determine what conditions led to the present state of affairs. Then we can assess the current environment to determine how these conditions have evolved or changed during the course of the downturn. With that in mind, let's go back to the spring of 2000, when the NASDAQ peaked, and see what led to the washout. We can identify three negative forces that began weighing heavily on the U.S. economy. For starters, our federal government was boasting a record budget surplus, somewhere in the neighborhood of $160 billion. You might ask, how could a budget surplus be negative? Simply stated, by accumulating a surplus, the government effectively pulls more from the economy than it actually needs to operate. This surplus represents real money that could have been creating economic activity rather

---

1 Journal of Financial Planning, John Walker CFP, July 2001 issue

than sitting idle in government coffers. Secondly, Alan Greenspan and the Federal Open Market Committee believed that our very healthy economy might lead to out-of-control inflation, so they began putting on the brakes by raising interest rates and pulling cash out of the system. The third drain was the rapidly increasing energy prices. Two dollars per gallon at the pump took quite a toll on the consumer. Dr. Robert Goodman, Putnam Investments' senior economic adviser, called these events the "perfect storm." [2] Just like the movie, all three storms merged together at precisely the same time, sending our economy into a tailspin and our stock market into the worst decline it's seen in almost three decades. So here we are, shell-shocked by the market downturn, wondering if we should continue investing or throw in the towel in favor of less volatile fixed income investments like bonds. Before we give up entirely, let's take a look at the way the three factors mentioned above have evolved to this point.

Mr. Greenspan, along with his crew, has cut interest rates an astonishing 11 times in the past 12 months. The budget surplus is all but gone due to the combination of last year's tax cut, together with military spending and rebuilding in the wake of the September 11 tragedy. Lastly, those once-high energy prices have fallen back to earth over the past few months. In essence, all three factors are at virtually opposite extremes compared to where they were at the market peak almost two years ago. I believe it's simply a matter of time before the major economic indicators begin reflecting a return to healthy, sustainable growth in the U.S. Positive economic activity leads to increased corporate earnings and ultimately to higher stock prices. A well-known motivational speaker once said, "If you want to be known as a great economist in America, predict growth. If you predict growth you'll be right 70% of the time, and if you're wrong temporarily, you'll be right pretty soon."

Now, let's take a step back and make sure we don't get carried away by this renewed optimism. First of all, in the short run, the water remains very murky. If you're looking for immediate gains, you could be sorely disappointed by this market, regardless of the present economic environment. Gambling in Las Vegas is as good a bet as the

---

2 Putnam Investment's Quarterly Economic Commentary, Goodman, Robert, January 2002

stock market in the short run. However, if you're patient and looking for long-term positive results, by all means consider stocks. Just be sure to diversify and never invest the money you'll need to spend in the near future.

In summary, the combination of the "energizing factor" and the overall improving economic fundamentals will likely lead to sustained growth and positive stock market results for the patient, long-term investor.

We didn't know in August of 2002, while the clouds were incredibly dark, that we were just seven months away from a dramatic stock market turnaround. As in so many of the articles you've read thus far, "Stock Market Mentality Part II" counsels the reader to hang in there and have faith that absolutely nothing lasts forever—that, in essence, the skies will clear and the market will rise again, which is precisely what began to happen in March of 2003.

Stock Market Mentality—Part 2
August 2002

A little over a year ago I wrote you a letter titled "Stock Market Mentality," in which I illustrated the most fundamental concept of investing: essentially taking an ownership position in an asset that is believed to have strong long-term potential for growth. Assets that might fit this description would include real estate, stocks, collectibles, and the like. In "Stock Market Mentality," we looked at the similarities between buying stocks (equities) and investing in real estate. In light of the current market environment, it seems timely to consider this comparison once again.

For starters, if someone had told me last year when we sent you "Stock Market Mentality" that the Standard & Poor's 500 and the NASDAQ Composite Indexes today would be down another 26.25% and 35.70% respectively (results from 3/15/2001 to 8/2/2002), I would have argued against it. Then again, if someone had told me in the mid-'90s how amazingly high the market would go by the end of the decade, I would have argued against that as well. I've heard it said that in the short run, the market is always motivated by either greed or fear and that it always overshoots when those emotions become extreme. In essence, the market overshot to the upside in the late '90s (greed) and presumably is overshooting to the downside in the early 2000s (fear). Nonetheless, here we are. So let's take another look at what I believe is the right perspective regarding the equity markets, regardless of whether the current trend is up or down.

Let's assume that you happen to be one of the countless individuals who have a good portion of your portfolio in equity mutual funds (If you're young, you justifiably may have the majority of your long-term portfolio in equities. If you're not so young, you'll likely have some exposure to equities but not nearly as much as the younger investor). If you held these positions in March of 2000, your funds are no doubt worth less now than they were at that time. You get those quarterly statements showing the dollar value dropping, and you say, "Hey, I didn't spend any money; where the heck did it go?" When all you receive as evidence of your investment is a paper valuation once per quarter, it may look no different to you than your bank statement. If your bank balance goes down, that means you spent some money that is gone forever. To get your balance back up, you have to deposit more money.

Now let's assume that instead of investing in the market you bought some real estate. No quarterly statement, just property that you have no intention of selling for another five, ten, or fifteen years. If the real estate market were down, you might know about it, but you wouldn't know exactly what your property is worth. However, you wouldn't be at all concerned, because you know that the real estate market goes through cycles. All indications are that you bought in a good location and you had absolutely no intention of selling this soon anyway. The value of the property at the moment is not important; it only matters that you sell it sometime later for more than you paid. In fact, if you're buying a little more as you go, you're actually getting more acres as the prices fall.

This concept is much like the ongoing investment in your 401(k) or the reinvestment of dividends and capital gains in your mutual funds. When prices are down, you buy more shares. The bottom line is that if you have faith that our economy and the investment markets are cyclical, you know that bear markets (like bull markets) don't last forever, even though they may seem to at times. Even after two and a half years, some forecasters still believe this bear market has more to run. They may be right, although I remember listening to many forecasters in March of 2000 who thought the bull market had much more upside room to run. For you and me, I say forget the short-term forecasts (positive or negative); we just need to remain diversified and be sure that our investment in equities is consistent with our personality and time horizon.

If you and I just returned from a two-and-a-half-year journey to Mars, and all that time we had no contact with Mother Earth, we'd see upon our return that the current economy looks to be in the early stages of recovery from a recent recession, that interest rates are at multi-decade lows, that business inventories have been steadily declining (suggesting companies will be spending money in the future to restock those shelves), and that the major averages are way off their all-time highs. And most importantly, we wouldn't have personally experienced this incredible bear market. With all this information, I wonder if we wouldn't be aggressive buyers of stocks. The problem is, having experienced this unstable period firsthand, it's hard to muster the courage to even stay in the market, let alone buy more.

Recently I pulled out some of the newsletters I was writing back in the late '90s when the market was skyrocketing. They had titles like "Why Buy Bonds" and "Managing Risk." At that time I was cautioning readers against believing that the bull market would last forever and emphasizing that diversifying among different asset classes is key to prudent investing. I'm sure that at some point in the future I'll look back at these more recent bear market newsletters and be compelled to tell you once again that the next bull market won't last forever—but, fortunately, neither will the next bear, just as the bear market of the early 2000s didn't last forever.

Please don't misunderstand; we'll never make a short-term forecast. For all I know, this bear market may take equities down even further. I'm very aware of all the problems out there, the biggie, of course, being the highly publicized misdeeds by certain higher-ups in corporate America. With the seemingly daily announcements of accounting irregularities, insider trading, and outright fraud, who in their right minds would by stocks now? Apparently not many, based on this year's stock market performance. Although I like how Warren Buffet put it in a recent interview with CNBC. He said, "The market is simply going through the necessary rinse cycle. During the rinse cycle all the dirt comes out, and what's left is clean laundry." The bottom line is, if the dirt is out there, it needs to be discovered and dealt with. Of course in the short-run the market may not like it, but in the long run it will no doubt make for a much healthier market.

My 13-year-old son said it best. Recently, after a couple of tough days for the market, he and I were in the car, and the radio news was reporting on the big sell-off. He asked me why stocks were going down so much. I, of course, took this opportunity to pass on to my young son some of the priceless wisdom gained from my 18 years in the financial services industry. I paused, then answered, "Uh, people are scared and selling their stocks." He replied, "Dad, that's crazy! It's the stock market; they should just wait for it to go back up!" I replied, "Son, you're wise beyond your years."

SECTION THREE

The Economy

"The Business Cycle" was written at the very end of the bear market of the early 2000s. This article takes a look at what led to the economic recession and bear market in stocks. And, through a little story I think you'll enjoy, it suggests that as unpleasant as they may be, economic contractions and stock market declines provide a much-needed cleansing that ultimately leads to the next expansion.

The Business Cycle
(The Forest through the Trees)
February 2003

Did you know that the Native American rain dances actually worked 100% of the time? That's right. The reason they never failed is that the Natives always kept dancing until it started raining.

For the past three years, this newsletter has played like a broken record—the same concepts, over and over again. Yes, I tried to wrap them in different packages, change a few words here and there, but when it came right down to it, I was always singing the same tune: if you're a long-term investor and can handle volatility, stay with a diversified portfolio consisting largely of common stocks and you'll do quite well in the end.

Well, here we are. We just suffered through the first three-year stretch of down markets in 60 years, and, believe it or not, there's no way I'm about to change my tune now. That would be akin to the rain dancers stopping dancing before it starts raining. Instead, we're going to take a walk through the business cycle to gain some perspective on where we've been and where we'll ultimately be in the future. We'll use the U.S. economy from 1991 to present as our illustration.

To begin with, the business cycle moves through very definite cycles of expansion and contraction. Expansions are periods of consistent economic growth, while contractions are periods when the economy shrinks. In between these cycles are periods referred to as peaks and troughs. The 1990s brought us the longest expansion in U.S. history. We experienced 10 solid years of uninterrupted economic growth fueled by billions of dollars flowing into the technology sector.

Finally, in March of 2001, the economy began contracting, and the record run was over.

What led to the end of the expansion? A number of developments that began to unfold in 2000 no doubt took their toll on the economy. Some factors were cyclical: the Fed raising interest rates in an attempt to ward off potential inflation (rising out of record economic growth) and the large budget surplus created by record tax revenues (the result of record employment and rising wages).

You may wonder how a budget surplus could be negative for the economy. A federal budget surplus simply means that the government collected revenue in excess of expenditures. In essence, the government received more in tax revenue than it had budgeted to spend, thus pulling more out of the economy than it put in. Or, put another way, taxes were too high. Other, non-cyclical factors, such as rapidly rising energy costs, also contributed to the economic downturn (at one point we were paying $2 per gallon at the pumps, and of course we all felt the incredible increases in our home utility bills). Add in the stock market's declines and the unthinkable tragedy of September 11, 2001 (which, of course, could never be discounted by any economic model), and you have the recipe for a doozy of a downturn.

So why such a long stock market decline? I guess you could say that the bear market in stocks has been proportionate to the preceding record-breaking bull market. Contractions, as painful as they seem, actually serve the very necessary purpose of cleansing the system of excesses born in the latter stages of an expansion. The expansion of the '90s created excesses beyond most growth periods of the past. There was such euphoria around the technology sector, and the benefits it brings to businesses and consumers alike, that it seemed the economic train could keep running for several more years before losing steam. The late '90s were characterized by record-low unemployment, consistent wage increases, generous employee stock programs, corporate mergers and acquisitions at an unprecedented pace (often funded by companies leveraging their own over-inflated stock), record-high corporate spending, and unbelievable pay packages for CEOs. And, oh yes, let's not forget Y2K.

Yes, that's right, Y2K. I know, nothing happened. Nobody froze up; the lights stayed on, and so forth. But in reality, Y2K did play an important role in the late '90s scenario. Just imagine how much money was spent on the technology needed to ensure that Y2K didn't turn out like the canned-food hoarders of the world thought it would (it's a good thing SpaghettiOs never spoil). That panicky tech spending no doubt produced record revenues for the tech providers (pushing their stocks to the moon) that in no way could be sustained when the threat was over.

Let's talk corruption. The faces of high-level corporate execs, some now facing possible prison terms, littered the covers of all the major financial publications. Multi-million-dollar salaries with incredible bonus programs were the norm for these geniuses. Just imagine, if you have more money than Fort Knox and your picture keeps showing up on the cover of *Forbes*, you're going to have an ego the size of Mt. Rushmore. Unfortunately, when egos swell, mistakes are made. And when huge egos make mistakes, mistakes get covered up. Evidence of declining profits gets lost in barbecued books cooked up by very clever accountants, swept under offshore rugs, and so on. Brokerage house analysts bend to the demands of their investment banking bosses, in essence touting worthless stocks because of the relationships these companies had with the investment banking side of their brokerage firm. When all this garbage came to the surface, investor confidence sank to the bottom. Add all this corruption to the excesses previously mentioned, and you get a very necessary, and painfully long, bear market. But take heart; ultimately all the resulting layoffs, plant closings, falling interest rates, etc. will lead to a much leaner and healthier corporate environment poised to take off when the inevitable next expansion begins.

Let's look at this economic cycle by relating it to my (not so) imaginary friend John. In the early '90s (the beginning of the great expansion), John (the U.S. economy) got his first job. He made decent money, spent and saved wisely, began raising a family, and bought his first home (early phases of expansion). Around the mid to late '90s, John experienced his mid-life crisis. He had begun to believe that he was truly something special (the beginning of the end). He had started his own company, which achieved immediate success. John just seemed to have a knack for making money, and loads of it. He became so confident in his ability to sustain his lifestyle, no matter what happened, that he began taking bigger and bigger risks. He quit coming home right after work. In fact, he kept coming home later and later. He consumed large quantities of pizza and chocolate cake daily. He took up drinking and gambling, even experimented with some illegal substances.

This went on for several years until finally on one fateful morning in March of 2002; John woke up with a pain in his chest (the end). He got scared and immediately went to see his doctor. After a brief exam, the doctor told John that he'd meet him at the hospital in 30 minutes; the ambulance was on its way. Eight tortuous hours later, the doctor sat on the edge of his hospital bed and asked what in the world was going on. John fessed up and his doctor let him have it. Oh the lecture, and the rhetorical query; did he really think he could get away with all the abuse he was laying on his body and mind in the late '90s? Did he truly believe this could go on forever? The doctor prescribed immediate drug and alcohol abuse treatment. He put him on a very strict diet and exercise regimen. John needed to lose around 150 pounds (plant closings, layoffs, etc.) and get his mental and spiritual life back in order. The doctor told him that fortunately he would survive. However, he's going to feel a lot of pain for at least the next three years, possibly longer (contraction). While he's rehabilitating, the authorities are going to arrest all the drug dealers (the corporate criminals and shady bookkeepers), so when he gets going again the bad guys won't be around to tempt him, at least not in the beginning. He'll feel great again, be very productive, grow at a healthy pace, and hopefully be much wiser for the experience.

And that, ladies and gentlemen, is how it works. Our economy goes through inevitable cycles of expansion and contraction—always has, always will. And so does the stock market. We just never know exactly what stage of the cycle we're in at any given time. That's why it's so important that we keep our heads about us when the cycle turns down. The next change in direction may be right around the corner, and, believe me, it usually comes when you least expect it.

The business cycle is the forest. The trees are all the day-to-day events that absorb our attention. Try to keep your focus on the forest, the bigger picture.

"Sitting on the Fence" pokes fun at the business of economic forecasting by introducing you to two economists, Ollie the Optimist and Perry the Pessimist, who can't seem to agree on our state of affairs in mid 2003, let alone where the economy may be headed from there. As it turns out, as I write this book (May 2006), Ollie seems to have had it right, at least to this point. Of course, due to the cyclical nature of our economy, all Perry has to do is stick to his guns and when the next inevitable recession hits, he can say, "See, I told you so."

Sitting on the Fence
August 2003

In our last newsletter you read my simplistic view of the business cycle. When I first sat down to write this current issue, my intent was to follow up with some commentary on where the economy appears to be headed today. Then I said to myself, "Marty, show a little humility. You're not an economist, so what qualifies you to offer commentary on the direction of the economy?" Therefore, in a humble attempt to get you some truly useful information, I did a little research to find out what real economists have to say about the current condition of our economy. What I found, I regret to report, was no real consensus, but rather somewhat dissenting opinions. As it turns out, some of today's economists are quite optimistic and others quite pessimistic about the present state of affairs (surprise, surprise). Isn't that interesting? (I'll offer my opinion on the reasons for the disagreement at the end of the article.) Since I can relate no consensus, I'll simply give you both sides of the fence.

Let's start with the pessimists' view, the opinion of economists who believe we still have big issues that will keep us mired in an economic funk for many months and possibly years to come. We'll call our pessimistic economist Perry. Perry believes that even though we've already experienced the most severe bear market in stocks since the Great Depression, as well as a recession in 2001, we ain't seen nuthin yet. He says the rapidly growing budget and trade deficits along with a declining U.S. dollar can only lead to higher interest rates and more pain down the road. Unemployment is steadily growing with no end in sight. The recent growth in auto and home sales is led purely by five-decade-low interest rates, which cannot be sustained under the weight of record deficits.

Perry contends that the recent rally in stocks is simply a technical bounce. There are still no real fundamentals to support higher stock prices going forward. Once the buyers, who have pushed this market higher, see the light, they'll sell in a blind panic that will send the Dow to levels that'll make 2002 look like a cakewalk. Another terrorist attack may happen at any moment, plunging our economy into a tailspin. And don't forget spiraling health care costs and the fact that many state governments are wrestling with record deficits of their own (most notably our own California). Perry preaches that the recently signed tax cut package will have no positive impact on the economy whatsoever. After all, the last one didn't do a thing. We still had our recession, didn't we? OK, Perry, I think we'd better stop here, since I'm seriously considering jumping out the window.

Let's now consider the optimist's point of view. Our optimistic economist's name is Ollie. Ollie believes in the business cycle. He says these last three years of pain have been the result of the record, and no doubt over-extended, economic expansion of the '90s, as well as the unsustainable bull market in stocks that came to a crashing halt in March of 2000. He says that this downturn is simply the necessary purging of the excesses created in the late '90s. He reminds us that, in the beginning stages of virtually every past expansion, unemployment actually rose before improving in later months. He argues that the recent record home and auto sales are the result not simply of low interest rates but also the desires of a huge baby-boom population entering their peak spending years.

Ollie is convinced that the bear market in stocks is over, or very close to it, and that the economy is poised for healthy growth ahead. He says U.S. corporations are much leaner, are more efficient, and will grow their earnings at a healthy pace as the economy continues to improve. The U.S. dollar's decline against major foreign currencies is just the thing U.S. exporters have been praying for; U.S. export sales increase as a falling dollar makes our goods less expensive to foreign buyers. He believes that the current tax cuts will put more money in people's hands that they'll immediately put to good use.

He challenges the critics who claim the last tax cut had no impact. He argues that things would have been dramatically worse in light of the bursting tech bubble, corporate corruption, the terrorist attack, the war in Iraq, extremely high oil prices, etc., had it not been for that very important tax relief. He reminds us that lower taxes always mean greater consumer spending, which means greater demand for goods and services, which leads to increased corporate profits, business spending, new jobs, and, as strange as it sounds, more taxes paid in the long run. That's right, lower taxes today mean greater tax revenue to the government in the future. This, Ollie says, is the way you remedy the federal and state budget problems. And lastly, Ollie is certain that this great bear market has created the kind of opportunity to buy under-priced stocks that comes but once in a lifetime.

So there you have it, both sides of the fence. But how, you may ask, can so many economists disagree on where the economy is headed? This, my friends, is a question I have pondered many a time over my 19-year career. You can take two equally qualified economists, the same age, from the same part of the country, educated at the same schools, and find them in complete opposition to one another when it comes to the direction of the economy.

How can this be? I believe there are three possible answers. One, they are basing their projections on different assumptions. Two, their optimism or pessimism is directly related to how often they were spanked as kids. Or three, they have different political affiliations. I'm hoping number one is the correct answer. But—please forgive my cynicism—I'm afraid in many instances it's number two or three. Number two suggests: once a pessimist always a pessimist, or once an optimist always an optimist. The forecast reflects the economist's personality. Number three suggests that some economists can be so committed to the success of their political party that their vision gets clouded when it comes to predicting our economic future. Who knows for sure?

Many a journalist and consumer alike voice a justifiable concern about the ever-expanding national debt. While I share this concern in a general sense, as you're about to read, I don't see the debt (as it stands today) as the crisis many would have us believe.

The Debate over the National Debt
December 2003

One of today's hottest political debates concerns the seriousness of the mounting national debt. The much-celebrated budget surplus disappeared almost concurrently with President Bush taking office. The bursting tech bubble and 9/11 did quite a number on the U.S. economy, resulting in lower tax revenue and higher government spending (much of it military related), which led to what is called cyclical deficit spending. In essence, the government borrows during an economic downturn in an effort to revive the economy and, in this instance, beef up national security. The administration's critics would have us believe that this round of deficit spending is irresponsible and will ultimately lead to financial ruin. The President's supporters preach that these actions are critical to our nation's long-term economic success.

The strength of the case against deficit spending lies in the widely held belief that a rising national debt will lead to dramatically higher interest rates, which is ultimately bad for the economy. And in some ways this makes sense. The law of supply and demand suggests that an increase in credit demand will increase its price, and/or that a rising national debt may cause the Fed to print more money to cover that cost, which would lead to higher inflation and higher interest rates down the line. However, as you read on, you'll see that the argument in favor of cyclical deficit spending may make some sense, as well.

The government currently owes its creditors approximately $3.5 trillion, and its debt is growing by the minute. This is a huge amount of money, but this number only amounts to a small percentage of the total credit market that determines interest rates. In the U.S. alone, businesses owe $7 trillion, state and local governments owe

$1.5 trillion, home mortgages total $8 trillion, and other consumer debt totals $1.6 trillion.

In today's global economy, one has to consider relevant debt in other nations, as well. Government debt in the Euro zone totals $5 trillion, and non-financial corporations and households owe $7 trillion. When you take into account the fact that money flows among Europe, the UK, Japan, Canada, and the U.S., there's a $50 trillion dollar market for debt. As you can see, the U.S. is only a small piece of a very big pie. Conceivably, our debt could expand by another $1 or $2 trillion and have very little, if any, impact on long-term interest rates.

Let's also look at a period in the past in which we were forced into deficit spending and see if, indeed, higher national debt led to higher interest rates. After World War II our national debt equaled 100% of GDP (much higher, in relative terms, than today's debt, which equals just 30% of our nation's production). But during that earlier period, long-term real interest rates remained quite low. If rising national debt leads to higher interest rates, one would have expected rates to go through the roof, post WWII.

Here's another way to look at it. The U.S. sports an $11 trillion economy. It's absolutely critical that, as a country, we do everything possible to support our national production. During periods of economic contraction, that production is in jeopardy. Therefore, it makes sense to find as many ways as possible (tax cuts, monetary stimulus, etc.) to stimulate consumer and business activity during sluggish times.

And lo and behold, something seems to be working. Our GDP was way up in the third quarter, and most other economic indicators have improved consistently throughout the year. The critics will confess that the numbers are improving, but they scream, "Where are all the jobs? This is a jobless recovery." I honestly wouldn't worry. History tells us very clearly that employment is a lagging indicator that virtually always improves later in the recovery. Don't be surprised if this time next year, the job numbers are showing noticeable improvement, as well.

And, by the way, expect interest rates to rise (at least modestly), not because of the national debt, but in response to an economy moving forward at a healthy pace.

In the spring of 2004, eight months before the presidential election, the U.S. job picture was one the collective media's hottest topics. The following article sheds some much-needed light on this very politically charged subject.

The Jobs Picture
March 2004

"Free Trade is killing us." "All our jobs are going outside the U.S." "How can this economic recovery produce more jobs when, everywhere you turn, more U.S. manufacturers are moving their operations overseas for the cheap labor?"

These are popular statements heard over backyard barbeques and on political debates seen on late night cable news programs. And trust me; I'm not here to argue against the reality that we have given up substantial employment to foreign workers. In fact, we've lost more than 2 million manufacturing jobs over the past 10 years alone. Manufacturing today accounts for just 11% of total U.S. employment, down dramatically from its peak of 35% in the 1950s.[1] However, I am here to help you put the jobs picture into its proper perspective.

You may be surprised, as I was, at the employment picture that develops when we consider the other key sectors of our economy. While manufacturing has seen steady job losses over the past decade, other areas have enjoyed steady job growth. Following are the results by sector:

Manufacturing	- 13.3%
Government (excluding education)	+ 5.6%
Retail	+14.5%
Total non-farm	+14.5%
Financial	+17.7%
Leisure	+22.7%
Health care	+26.8%
Educational services	+28.2%

---

1 U.S. Department of Labor's 'Bureau of Labor Statistics' Nov. 2003

| Professional and business services | +38.5% |
| Construction | +40.7% |

The new jobs created in education services alone were greater than all the jobs lost in the manufacturing sector over the past decade.

Considering the bigger picture, it's obvious that our economic future is not simply being sold to the lowest bidder, as one might think, given the manufacturing numbers. However, it appears that our overall employment has seen very definite improvement as the U.S. economy has evolved into the largest provider of services on the planet.

From a historical perspective, the current figures aren't necessarily all that bad, either. After the corporate profits meltdown we experienced during the early 2000s, national unemployment sits at just around 6%. But what about wages? We may have seen a net increase in jobs over the past decade, but are those new jobs paying as much as the jobs lost? There are more people working, but aren't they making a lot less money? There are no doubt numerous instances in which a worker has had to take a lower-paying position or face unemployment due to operations being moved abroad. Considering the bigger picture, however, the jobs with the above-average growth over the past decade actually pay slightly higher wages than those with below-average growth (according to the Department of Labor).

Now, make no mistake; there are some very real risks that lie in waiting for us as we go forward. We can certainly talk about high energy costs, potentially higher interest rates, the threat of terrorism, the rising cost of health care, and so forth, any or all of which could slow the rate of economic growth in the future. However, it's very important that we see the reality that underlies the headlines. We can only do this by considering all the pertinent facts, whether we're talking about the national debt or the current trends in employment.

Speaking of headlines, get ready! 2004 will feature a politically charged media circus the likes of which we've never seen. The rhetoric on both sides of the political fence will reach a fever pitch. One side will be telling us we're seeing improvement and the future is very bright, and the other will preach that we're going to a hot place in a hand basket. Reality is always somewhere in between.

Like the previous article, "The Truth on Trade" touches on a very politically sensitive subject that, when viewed through an unbiased lens, may not nearly be the potential cataclysm some might have us believe.

The Truth on Trade
July 2004

Our ever-expanding trade deficit (U.S. exports vs. imports), like at least one other major economic statistic (the national debt), at first blush can paint a very daunting picture. However, when we look below the surface, searching for the proper perspective, we often discover that things aren't always as they appear. In this article we'll take a look at some key statistics that I believe shed a new light on what is arguably the most politically sensitive economic indicator.

In March of this year, the trade imbalance reached a record-breaking $46 billion, which put pressure on the U.S. dollar and fueled protectionist sentiments. It seems perfectly fair to say that if we import that much more than we export, we are losing to our foreign competition. The question I'm posing here is, does our conventional method of measuring foreign trade tell the whole story? I'm convinced it doesn't.

Where the current method of measuring trade grossly misses the mark is in its ignorance of activity generated by U.S.-based multinational companies (American companies with foreign operations). According to *Business Week*[11], these companies account for 25% of U.S. gross domestic product and 20% of U.S. employment. In 2001, 77% of the multinationals' global production, 80% of their capital spending, and 74% of their global employment occurred right here in the U.S. From 1991 to 2001, for every three overseas jobs they created, five were created in the U.S. These companies are also major traders. In 2001, they accounted for 58% of U.S. exports vs. 38% of U.S imports.

The extent to which U.S. multinationals rely on their own foreign operations to sell goods and services to other countries is the statistic that most supports the notion that we should reevaluate

---

1 Business Week, Weekly Finance Column, 7 June 2004

how we measure trade. According to Rebecca McCaughrin, a Morgan Stanley economist, foreign sales through companies located in other countries, but owned by U.S. multinationals, generated $17.7 trillion in sales in 2002, more than double the global exports of about $8 trillion[1]. Today, global sales by foreign affiliates of U.S. corporations are roughly three times as large as total U.S. exports. As you can see, if the trade deficit were recalculated, adding these sales as U.S. exports, a very different picture would emerge.

The fact of the matter is that these companies are establishing their foreign operations not to exploit low wage opportunities overseas only to sell the goods back to us, but rather to sell to foreign markets in the most efficient manner. In fact, more than 60% of employment created by foreign affiliates of U.S. multinationals occurred in high-wage countries, such as those in Europe, and roughly 66% of their sales went to customers living in the countries where the affiliates were located; 24% went to other foreign markets, and only 11% of sales went to U.S. customers. In essence, the foreign affiliates were created to get closer to other markets as opposed to making their goods cheaply, only to send them back to the U.S.[1]

I know this flies in the face of popular opinion as it relates our huge trade deficit, but (as with a few other economic concerns) if we simply scratch the surface a little, we might find that things aren't that bad after all.

In "Oil vs. the Stock Market," make note of the reference to oil at $50 per barrel back in the fall of 2004. I suggested that then, had I known oil would rise so high , I would have predicted real trouble for the stock market. Yet here we sit today (summer 2006) with oil at $75 per barrel and the market is hanging in there. Had I been thinking$75 per barrel terms, I would have told you that a major bear market was all but inevitable. However, a funny thing happened on the way to $75 per barrel: the Dow Jones Industrial Average went from 9,933 on October 16, 2004 (the day I wrote the following article) to 11,284 (today). Of course, a bear market in our future is all but inevitable—in fact, as you read in previous articles, bear markets are healthy cyclical phenomena. But perhaps as you'll read below, oil doesn't necessarily have to be the catalyst.

Oil vs. the Stock Market
October 2004

If you had told me a year ago that oil prices would be at $40 a barrel today, let alone $50+, I would have told you the Dow Jones Industrial Average would be a lot closer to 8,000 than 10,000 (where it currently sits today). After all, the last time we saw oil prices anywhere near these levels was in the early 1970s, during the Arab Oil Embargo. The resulting bear market of 1973 and 1974 was, at the time, the worst since the Great Depression. There is no mystery about why high oil prices can lead to lower stock prices. Basically, if energy costs use up a disproportionate amount of our liquidity, there's less cash for businesses to spend on new technology and less for the consumer to splurge with at Wal-Mart on the weekend. And less spending means lower corporate earnings and ultimately lower stock prices.

So what's going on this time around? Oil prices are at record highs, but the market is only off slightly (as of 10/15, the Dow is down 2.1%, the S&P 500 is up 0.92%, and the NASDAQ Composite Index is down 5.32%). Well, apparently our economy functions somewhat differently than it did in the '70s. Just yesterday the Federal Reserve Chairman, Alan Greenspan, speaking to an audience in New York City on the current oil market and its impact on the economy, stated that, thanks to technological innovation, we are only half as dependant on oil as we were in the '70s. He estimated that the record ascent of oil prices has only reduced this year's GDP by 0.75%.

An article titled, "How the U.S. Is Riding Out the Energy Storm,"[1] in next week's *Business Week* magazine, predicts that real GDP will grow at a very healthy 4%, or better, for all of 2004. Mr. Greenspan believes innovation will continue, further reducing our dependency on oil in the long-run, and that many of the short-term dynamics pushing prices higher (bad weather in the Gulf of Mexico, oil worker strikes in Nigeria, the coming cold winter months, the financials struggles with Russia's largest oil producer, and so on) will work themselves out in the not-too-distant future. However, the longer-term issues facing the oil market (Middle East tensions, growing global demand, etc.) suggest we won't likely see $20 a barrel anytime soon. One other interesting point to ponder, according to Mr. Greenspan, is that even above $50 a barrel, oil is actually much cheaper than it was in the early 1980s, when adjusted for inflation. If oil prices simply rose in line with the Consumer Price Index, today's price would be $80 to $85/barrel.

I've heard a few people comment that oil industry fat cats are raking in a bundle at the expense of the world's energy consumers— and at the extreme, there have even been a few conspiracy theories floating around. No doubt oil companies are seeing record earnings in the short run, and they may be loving every minute of it. But trust me, these "fat cats" are also long-term thinkers, and they know full well that the longer oil stays at these levels or higher, the more quickly alternative sources will hit the market. They'd be shooting themselves in the proverbial foot if they were truly manufacturing prices above what the fundamentals would dictate.

So what should we expect in the near term? As relates to oil, unfortunately, I'd say, more of the same. With an anticipated cold winter approaching and global demand remaining high, oil prices are not likely to retreat measurably until next spring. And consequently, stocks have a somewhat steep mountain to climb. The good news is

1 Business Week, How the U.S. Is Riding Out the Energy Storm, 18 October 2004

that liquidity remains very high. Corporate balance sheets look very clean with plenty of cash to spend when the coast is clearer. And consumers have held up amazing well. There's no doubt that the aggressive stimulus (recent tax cuts) and record low interest rates have served to hold this economy up under the weight of all this uncertainty.

To succeed in this market, we'll have to remain very patient and anticipate unusually high volatility. History has taught us that things always have a way of working themselves out over time. As for bonds, I'm still suggesting we play it safe and keep maturities very short. Interest rates do move in cycles, and we are just coming off of fifty-year lows. As interest rates rise, the long end of the bond market will likely see a very noticeable decline in value. But for the moment, high oil prices (which slow economic growth) are not only keeping a lid on the stock market but on interest rates as well. Again, in this environment, patience is the key.

Here's yet another politically sensitive topic that, when viewed from all angles, isn't quite as bad as some would portray it to be. Not to suggest that a nation's currency declining in value is all good, but, as you're about to read, it's not all bad, either.

The Falling Dollar
December 2004

Just a few weeks ago I offered some insight into what, at the time, was the dominant topic in the investment media—high oil prices. While oil is still a hot topic, it has fallen to second place on the current worry list, behind the weak U.S. dollar. We've heard a number of economists and investment "experts" bemoan the fact that the almighty dollar seems to be losing its luster, and at this moment, it takes $1.33 to equal one Euro. I can recall when you could get a Euro for just around $.80 (that's a 66% difference). So what's causing the decline, and what does it really mean? Does it spell ultimate economic collapse, or are there some benefits to be had?

First of all, to answer the "what's causing it?" question, we must understand that the dollar is just like any other commodity. When in high demand the value rises, and when in low demand the value declines. It's no secret that we import substantially more goods than we export each month (witness the trade deficit). Also, due to the recession and the war on terrorism, the federal budget deficit hit all-time highs in 2003 and 2004, forcing the Treasury to issue bonds at a heightened pace to finance our expenditures.

The negative view of a falling dollar suggests that, if it continues, foreign investors may tire of seeing their U.S. investments lose value and ultimately sell, creating a free-falling dollar. At that point, interest rates would rise dramatically, our real estate boom would bust, bond prices would drop, and the stock market would recede faster than a 42-year-old investment adviser's hairline. To make matters even worse, a falling dollar makes foreign imports more expensive for U.S. consumers.

As dire as this sound, there's a bright silver lining to a falling dollar. While the dollar declines, foreign currencies rise, and U.S. goods become very competitive in foreign lands. In fact, at the moment, the biggest complaints are coming from our overseas competitors, while our own multinational companies are singing from the rooftops. Rising overseas sales lead to greater profits, which lead ultimately to more jobs, higher wages, higher stock prices, a lower trade deficit, and more internal revenue (thus lowering the budget deficit).

So, in essence, the so-called "weak dollar" may not be as problematic as it sounds. At a minimum, it provides a trade advantage that could ultimately be very good for the U.S. economy. In the end, the financial markets will decide on the correct price for the dollar. What we should hope for is a level that allows our companies to compete in the global marketplace without scaring off the foreign inflows that we rely on so heavily.

As for a potential mass sell-off, I for one would place the likelihood very low. The U.S. remains the largest and most stable economy in the world. Our GDP is expected to come in at a healthy 4% growth rate this year and is projected to grow at about the same pace in 2005. It's hard to imagine that, at the dollar's current low levels, foreign investors would want to unload their U.S. holdings in a big way. In fact, my guess is that the smart money is beginning to see the dollar as a serious investment opportunity.

So where do we go from here? In the weeks ahead, our friends overseas will complain more vigorously that the U.S. is ignoring the falling dollar in favor of an improving trade deficit. And I think they're right; it's unlikely that the U.S. will step into the currency markets and attempt to prop up the dollar anytime soon. The economy's recent performance has been positive, and for that reason alone, there's a very good chance that Alan Greenspan and the Federal Open Market Committee will continue to increase rates, which should provide some support for the dollar, at least in the short run.

"Tax Cuts and Tax Revenue" explores the backward-sounding notion that tax cuts can ultimately lead to increased tax revenue. Strange as it may sound, there may very well be something to it, as you're about to read.

Tax Cuts and Tax Revenue
October 2005

Today we're going to focus on everyone's favorite topic, taxes—specifically, the faulty notion that a reduction in tax rates must correspondingly reduces tax receipts.

Yes, I do mean the *faulty* notion. At first blush, you might think that if you lower the tax rate applied to household and corporate income, you end up with less tax collected. Therefore the current administration was an easy target for the class-warfare lobby when it narrowly passed major tax cuts back in 2003. The centerpiece of this legislation was a reduction in the tax rate on dividends to 15% (from 39%) and capital gains tax rates to 15% (from 20%). The proponents of this legislation promised that lower taxes would in fact provide a stimulus to the economy so strong that the result would be higher corporate profits (which, by the way, are a good thing for everyone), more jobs, higher overall economic growth, and, consequently, greater tax receipts. While the opponents cried foul, suggesting that the tax cuts were only for the very rich and that cutting taxes at a time when the economy was licking its recessionary wounds would be fiscally irresponsible.

Well, here we are, two years later, and lo and behold—federal tax receipts are almost off the chart. In June, the Congressional Budget Office released its latest report on tax revenue, and the numbers were astounding. In the first eight months of this fiscal year, federal tax receipts jumped by $187 billion, or 15% over those collected in 2004. In the two years since the tax cut, tax receipts from corporations and individuals are up 30%. Business spending on capital purchases is up a huge 22%, reversing the slump that gripped our economy in 2001 and 2002. And as a result—until the last, hurricane-ravaged month—job numbers have been rising steadily (a huge benefit to the middle-income American).

In essence, it works! Lower tax rates stimulate economic growth, resulting in higher tax revenue. Unfortunately, the dividend and capital gain tax cuts are set to expire in 2008, unless they are made permanent as the administration has proposed. But of course the opponents are completely undeterred by the data. They are charging that we can't afford to make the cuts permanent, that in light of all that our nation is facing at the moment, we must allow the cuts to expire and get the rates back up to the pre-2003 levels. I would suggest that, based on what we've seen in the last two years, we cannot afford to let them expire.

If there's a reason to criticize the current administration (from a fiscal standpoint), it's for the rate at which it is spending the revenue. The Congressional Budget Office also reported that federal expenditures are up $110 billion, or 7.2% so far this year (as of June). I'm not sure what the solution is, but again, I'm quite sure of what the solution is not: it is not the reversing of legislation that has clearly brought economic growth and greater revenue at a time when we need it most.

Levying tariffs on imported goods can be a very effective way for politicians to make nice with domestic industry. However, as I explain below, what's good for the goose isn't always good for the gander.

Tariffs—Are They Good for the U.S.?
October 2006

In this article, we're tackling a very politically charged aspect of international trade: the idea that if a country's policy-makers—in an effort to support one of their own industries (and seemingly their country's workforce as a whole)—levies a duty, or tariff, on goods imported from another country, their own country would be rewarded for the effort. Or, more simply put, the idea that making foreign goods less competitive (more expensive) in the U.S. serves the greater good of the American citizen.

At first glance, you might strongly agree; if we help out one of our own by making our benefactor's overseas competition less competitive, we're supporting U.S. industry, which has to be good for the U.S. consumer. And there's no doubt that such a move would certainly benefit one of our own industries. More product would be sold, more workers would be hired, their pay would increase, they'd spend more money, and so on. What could possibly be wrong with this picture?

I realize I'm taking a risk here. For many Americans, foreign trade is a very sensitive subject, so I apologize in advance if this article strikes a nerve or two. However, I'm still going to offer the perspective that what we see on the surface may not carry quite the benefit we might think, once we dig a little deeper.

Again, on the surface, if we create higher prices on imported goods by adding a tariff, bringing the price in line with the same goods domestically produced, we (the U.S. manufacturers) win, and the foreign producer loses. Yes, that's correct. But we must realize that not all U.S. manufacturers win; since the tariff only directly benefits the manufacturers of the particular item involved, one could argue that not only does it not benefit other U.S. producers, it may actually hurt them.

As implied, the foreign competitor is not the only loser—there's the U.S. citizen who would have paid less for the same (imported) product had the tariff not been attached. So the U.S. consumers lose, in a very direct way. If they had the opportunity to pay less for the item in question, they would have had money left over to go to the movies, buy some new shoes and new lights for the house, save for a vacation, pay college tuition for their kids, etc., etc. Wow, when you stop and think about it, there are lots of potential losers, considering all the producers who won't see those extra dollars.

But, to be fair, we must back up and focus on the industry being aided by the tariff. As stated previously, this industry's fortune should translate into increased economic activity as these earnings are allocated to employee paychecks (and increased personal spending), increased business investment, etc. So one could compromise and say that the ultimate impact of the tariff is neutral. The overall economy benefits just the same, but the initial stimulus created by these dollars comes directly from the industry benefiting from the tariff, rather than from the general population, as implied above.

However, we then must consider the economic impact of losing a potential foreign customer. That's right, what about the foreign producer who would have earned U.S. dollars on the un-tariffed product? Ultimately, U.S. dollars have to be spent in the U.S. Perhaps that foreign producer was a big buyer of computers and related technology produced by U.S. manufacturers. Now, because of the tariff, the foreign buyer takes his business elsewhere and our U.S. manufacturers suffer. Of course, we can hope that the benefit to the U.S. industry protected by the tariff translates into greater domestic demand for the products that would have been sold to the foreign producers hit by the tariff. If so, no harm, no foul.

One last question—what if the foreign producers are big buyers of U.S. treasury bonds? If their revenue suffers due to the tariff, there's less money to flow back to our treasury market, possibly forcing interest rates higher. Once again, we'd have to count on the U.S. producers aided by the tariff to make the difference there, as well.

It seems quite obvious that in the final analysis, *at best*, the tariff's immediate result is neither a positive nor a negative when it comes to the economy as whole.

I think it fitting that this book's namesake be its last article. And I hope that, as we step into the future, whatever it may hold, you trust that, ultimately, an even brighter future awaits this generation and those to come.

Making Lemonade
April 2005

After 21 years of reading and listening to the financial news media report on all that is, was, and may be, I've come to realize that there is a silver lining to many of the seemingly negative events that occur in our world. So, for this letter, rather than offer my perspective on the latest development, I'll offer you a positive perspective on a handful of the "negative" events (or developments) of the past few years. In other words, let's make lemonade out of some of life's lemons.

The bursting tech bubble/stock market plunge—2000 through 2002

Lemon—In the spring of 2000, just when even the most conservative investor threw caution to the wind (perhaps bought an Internet stock or two), tech stocks began a three-year plunge like nothing the market's seen since the Great Depression. Thousands of jobs were lost while tech and Internet companies were dropping like flies. When the dust settled, the tech-heavy NASDAQ Index lost 80% of its value.

Lemonade—If the bubble hadn't burst, the legitimate companies may not have had to take a long, hard look at themselves and get back to their core competencies—in essence, get back to what they do best and most profitably. If the bubble hadn't burst, Alan Greenspan and the Federal Open Market Committee may not have had to pump cash into the economy and force interest rates to record lows in order to get the economy back on track. And therefore the housing market boom—which probably pushed your net worth through the roof (pardon the pun)—fueled largely by fifty-year-low mortgage rates, may not have occurred. Consumers would not have been able to refinance their mortgages at much lower rates, allowing them to improve their lifestyles, pay off other debt, and save more toward retirement and their kids' college educations. And trust me, corporate balance sheets would not look nearly as healthy as they do today if the tech bubble had never burst.

Corporate scandals 2000–?

Lemon—A huge number of employees of companies like Enron, MCI, and Global Crossing, to name a few, lost their entire life savings by believing the outright lies their employers told. The employees were told their companies were thriving in a perpetual never-never land of milk and honey, and if they invested all of their 401(k) accounts in company stock, they'd be richly rewarded. As these bloated companies began to buckle beneath the weight of their own excesses, the executives sold their personal company stock, while continuing the hype to their own unsuspecting employees and lying to Wall Street and the IRS about what was really developing below the surface.

Lemonade—If this corruption had not been brought to light, the bad guys may not have been caught. And the penalties for corporate fraud would not have gone up dramatically (just the other day, one former chief executive officer of a large telecom company was found guilty on all counts and now faces a possible life sentence). And tomorrow's executives would not have learned that "cooking the books" doesn't pay. And companies would not be adopting stricter accounting standards, as they are today in increasing numbers, so that we can be confident that what we're seeing is truly what we're getting. And, lastly, the individual investor would not have learned a very valuable lesson: never, never, never put all your eggs in any one basket!

The national debt

Lemon—The government currently owes its creditors $3.5+ trillion, and the figure is growing by the minute. The law of supply and demand suggests that an increase in credit demand will increase its price and/or that a rising national debt may cause the Fed to print more money to cover that cost, which would lead to higher inflation and higher interest rates down the line. All of this seems to be very bad news for the U.S. economy!

Lemonade—In reality, history offers virtually no proof that high national debt leads to high interest rates. In fact, when we take a look at a period when deficit spending created a national that equaled 100% of our Gross Domestic Produce (today's national debt equals 30% of GDP) — just after World War II, we find that, during the entire period, long-term interest rates remained very low. If high national debt levels indeed lead to high interest rates, we certainly should have seen interest rates rise dramatically, post WWII. But they didn't, not even a little. Currently, rates are on the rise, but not because of deficit spending, but because our economy is growing at a pace that is inspiring the Federal Open Market Committee to nudge rates higher, keeping potential inflation at bay.

That said, we should always keep a watchful eye on our national debt. There is no doubt a level where the debt burden would become a true burden on the economy, particularly during contractions.

The weak U.S. dollar

Lemon—Substantially more U.S. dollars are flowing to foreign lands than there are foreign dollars coming to the U.S., forcing the dollar to lose value relative to non-U.S. currencies. And if this trend continues, foreign investors may tire of seeing their U.S. investments lose value and ultimately sell, creating a free-falling dollar. At that point, interest rates would rise dramatically, our real estate boom would bust, bond prices would drop, and the stock market would take a hit that would make the bursting tech bubble feel like a walk in the park. To make matters even worse, a falling dollar makes foreign imports more expensive for U.S. consumers.

Lemonade—While the dollar declines, foreign currencies rise and U.S. goods become very competitive in foreign lands. In fact, at the moment, the biggest complaints are coming from our overseas competitors, while our own multinational companies are singing from the rooftops. Rising overseas sales lead to greater profits, which lead ultimately to more jobs, higher wages, higher stock prices, a lower trade deficit, and more internal revenue (lowering the budget deficit). Today's weak dollar is more a product of a healthier U.S. economy than of foreign economies. U.S. consumers have discretionary income and an appetite for goods from all over the world. In short, more money is flowing out of the U.S. than coming in, largely because the U.S. consumer has more money to spend.

That said, a forever declining currency would speak poorly of a nation and would indeed become problematic, exacerbating the issues raised above.

Rising oil prices

Lemon—As I write this letter, oil costs $57 a barrel. Unbelievable! With high energy costs using up a disproportionate amount of our liquidity, there's less cash for businesses to spend on new technology and less for the consumer to splurge with at Wal-Mart on the weekend. And less spending means lower corporate earnings and ultimately lower stock prices.

Lemonade—I'm climbing out on a limb on this one, but I have to say that probably the best thing to happen to the world, from an energy perspective, is the escalating price of a barrel of oil. Yes, I said it: near-record-high oil prices right now may very well be what's best for us all in the long run. Without this current "crisis," auto companies would have no reason to rush to produce more fuel-efficient cars (hybrids and the like). The current push to discover oil in parts of the world other than the Middle East would not be necessary (I have to believe that we'd be better off not depending so heavily on that part of the world for our energy supply). And last but not least, we wouldn't be so desperate to develop alternative fuel sources. Even the environment wins!

In closing, the next time the stock market tumbles, oil prices shoot up, or another unexpected event sends a shock wave through the economy, keep the faith and understand that, in all likelihood, something good may ultimately come of it. The harshest winters always lead to the most beautiful springs.

EPILOGUE

Here's a simple little story from the *Tao Te Ching*, written in 550 BC, that I'd like you to ponder.

> There's a farmer whose son broke his leg. The villagers came to the farmer and said, "My! That's a great misfortune. Your son has broken his leg; now he can't help you in the fields." The farmer replied, "It is neither a fortune nor a misfortune." A day later, the government troops came to the village looking for young men to conscript into the army. They had to leave the boy behind because of his broken leg.
>
> Then one day the farmer's horse jumped the fence and ran away. The villagers came to him and said, "What a great misfortune that your horse ran away." The farmer replied, "It is neither a fortune nor a misfortune." A couple days later, the horse came home with a dozen wild horses following behind. The villagers came to him and said, "It's a great fortune that your horse came back with twelve others." He of course replied, "It is neither a fortune nor a misfortune."

The farmer's attitude toward life's inevitable events is the very same that today's successful investor applies to economic and market events. The farmer understood that (like the market) the world may deal us a few surprises during our lifetimes (if we're lucky), but the key to living a peaceful life is to never judge the hands we're dealt.

Consider once again the study highlighted in this book's forward, and understand that long-term investment success is not hard to achieve. Ironically, just about the only way to fail is to *try too hard*.

I wish you all the success, joy, and riches (lemonade) life has to offer.

www.ingramcontent.com/pod-product-compliance
Lightning Source LLC
Chambersburg PA
CBHW030854180526
45163CB00004B/1577